THE
YUMA

THE
YUMA

Robert L. Bee
University of Connecticut

Frank W. Porter III
General Editor

CHELSEA HOUSE PUBLISHERS
New York   Philadelphia

Pe

On the cover   Clay dolls, about 7″ high, made in the
late 19th century. Their painted decoration represents
Yuma body tattooing and painting.

Chelsea House Publishers
Editor-in-Chief   Nancy Toff
Executive Editor   Remmel T. Nunn
Managing Editor   Karyn Gullen Browne
Copy Chief   Juliann Barbato
Picture Editor   Adrian G. Allen
Art Director   Maria Epes
Manufacturing Manager   Gerald Levine

Indians of North America
Senior Editor   Marjorie P. K. Weiser

Staff for **THE YUMA**
Associate Editor   Liz Sonneborn
Copy Editor   Lisa Fenev
Deputy Copy Chief   Ellen Scordato
Editorial Assistant   Claire M. Wilson
Designer   Donna Sinisgalli
Picture Researcher   Marion Bodine
Production Coordinator   Joseph Romano

First Printing

1 3 5 7 9 8 6 4 2

Library of Congress Cataloging-in-Publication Data

Bee, Robert L.
The Yuma / Robert L. Bee : Frank W. Porter III, general editor.
   p.   cm.—(Indians of North America)
Bibliography: p.
Includes index.
Summary: Examines the culture, history, and changing
fortunes of the Yuma Indians.
ISBN 1-55546-737-7.
     0-7190-0403-1 (pbk.)
1. Yuma Indians. [1. Yuma Indians. 2. Indians of North
America.] I. Porter, Frank W., 1947– . II. Title. III. Series:
Indians of North America (Chelsea House Publishers)
E99.Y94B44   1989   88-39463
973'.0497—dc19   CIP
                                                                AC

CONTENTS

INDIANS OF NORTH AMERICA

CHELSEA HOUSE PUBLISHERS

INDIANS OF NORTH AMERICA: CONFLICT AND SURVIVAL

Frank W. Porter III

The Indians survived our open intention of wiping them out, and since the tide turned they have even weathered our good intentions toward them, which can be much more deadly.

John Steinbeck
America and Americans

When Europeans first reached the North American continent, they found hundreds of tribes occupying a vast and rich country. The newcomers quickly recognized the wealth of natural resources. They were not, however, so quick or willing to recognize the spiritual, cultural, and intellectual riches of the people they called Indians.

The Indians of North America examines the problems that develop when people with different cultures come together. For American Indians, the consequences of their interaction with non-Indian people have been both productive and tragic. The Europeans believed they had "discovered" a "New World," but their religious bigotry, cultural bias, and materialistic world view kept them from appreciating and understanding the people who lived in it. All too often they attempted to change the way of life of the indigenous people. The Spanish conquistadores wanted the Indians as a source of labor. The Christian missionaries, many of whom were English, viewed them as potential converts. French traders and trappers used the Indians as a means to obtain pelts. As Francis Parkman, the 19th-century historian, stated, "Spanish civilization crushed the Indian; English civilization scorned and neglected him; French civilization embraced and cherished him."

7

Nearly 500 years later, many people think of American Indians as curious vestiges of a distant past, waging a futile war to survive in a Space Age society. Even today, our understanding of the history and culture of American Indians is too often derived from unsympathetic, culturally biased, and inaccurate reports. The American Indian, described and portrayed in thousands of movies, television programs, books, articles, and government studies, has either been raised to the status of the "noble savage" or disparaged as the "wild Indian" who resisted the westward expansion of the American frontier.

Where in this popular view are the real Indians, the human beings and communities whose ancestors can be traced back to ice-age hunters? Where are the creative and indomitable people whose sophisticated technologies used the natural resources to ensure their survival, whose military skill might even have prevented European settlement of North America if not for devastating epidemics and disruption of the ecology? Where are the men and women who are today diligently struggling to assert their legal rights and express once again the value of their heritage?

The various Indian tribes of North America, like people everywhere, have a history that includes population expansion, adaptation to a range of regional environments, trade across wide networks, internal strife, and warfare. This was the reality. Europeans justified their conquests, however, by creating a mythical image of the New World and its native people. In this myth, the New World was a virgin land, waiting for the Europeans. The arrival of Christopher Columbus ended a timeless primitiveness for the original inhabitants.

Also part of this myth was the debate over the origins of the American Indians. Fantastic and diverse answers were proposed by the early explorers, missionairies, and settlers. Some thought that the Indians were descended from the Ten Lost Tribes of Israel, others that they were descended from inhabitants of the lost continent of Atlantis. One writer suggested that the Indians had reached North America in another Noah's ark.

A later myth, perpetrated by many historians, focused on the relentless persecution during the past five centuries until only a scattering of these "primitive" people remained to be herded onto reservations. This view fails to chronicle the overt and covert ways in which the Indians successfully coped with the intruders.

All of these myths presented one-sided interpretations that ignored the complexity of European and American events and policies. All left serious questions unanswered. What were the origins of the American Indians? Where did they come from? How and when did they get to the New World? What was their life—their culture—really like?

In the late 1800s, anthropologists and archaeologists in the Smithsonian Institution's newly created Bureau of American Ethnology in Washington,

D.C., began to study scientifically the history and culture of the Indians of North America. They were motivated by an honest belief that the Indians were on the verge of extinction and that along with them would vanish their languages, religious beliefs, technology, myths, and legends. These men and women went out to visit, study, and record data from as many Indian communities as possible before this information was forever lost.

By this time there was a new myth in the national consciousness. American Indians existed as figures in the American past. They had performed a historical mission. They had challenged white settlers who trekked across the continent. Once conquered, however, they were supposed to accept graciously the way of life of their conquerors.

The reality again was different. American Indians resisted both actively and passively. They refused to lose their unique identity, to be assimilated into white society. Many whites viewed the Indians not only as members of a conquered nation but also as "inferior" and "unequal." The rights of the Indians could be expanded, contracted, or modified as the conquerors saw fit. In every generation, white society asked itself what to do with the American Indians. Their answers have resulted in the twists and turns of federal Indian policy.

There were two general approaches. One way was to raise the Indians to a "higher level" by "civilizing" them. Zealous missionaries considered it their Christian duty to elevate the Indian through conversion and scanty education. The other approach was to ignore the Indians until they disappeared under pressure from the ever-expanding white society. The myth of the "vanishing Indian" gave stronger support to the latter option, helping to justify the taking of the Indians' land.

Prior to the end of the 18th century, there was no national policy on Indians simply because the American nation has not yet come into existence. American Indians similarly did not possess a political or social unity with which to confront the various Europeans. They were not homogeneous. Rather, they were loosely formed bands and tribes, speaking nearly 300 languages and thousands of dialects. The collective identity felt by Indians today is a result of their common experiences of defeat and/or mistreatment at the hands of whites.

During the colonial period, the British crown did not have a coordinated policy toward the Indians of North America. Specific tribes (most notably the Iroquois and the Cherokee) became military and political pawns used by both the crown and the individual colonies. The success of the American Revolution brought no immediate change. When the United States acquired new territory from France and Mexico in the early 19th century, the federal government wanted to open this land to settlement by homesteaders. But the Indian tribes that lived on this land had signed treaties with European governments assuring their title to the land. Now the United States assumed legal responsibility for honoring these treaties.

At first, President Thomas Jefferson believed that the Louisiana Purchase contained sufficient land for both the Indians and the white population. Within a generation, though, it became clear that the Indians would not be allowed to remain. In the 1830s the federal government began to coerce the eastern tribes to sign treaties agreeing to relinquish their ancestral land and move west of the Mississippi River. Whenever these negotiations failed, President Andrew Jackson used the military to remove the Indians. The southeastern tribes, promised food and transportation during their removal to the West, were instead forced to walk the "Trail of Tears." More than 4,000 men, woman, and children died during this forced march. The "removal policy" was successful in opening the land to homesteaders, but it created enormous hardships for the Indians.

By 1871 most of the tribes in the United States had signed treaties ceding most or all of their ancestral land in exchange for reservations and welfare. The treaty terms were intended to bind both parties for all time. But in the General Allotment Act of 1887, the federal government changed its policy again. Now the goal was to make tribal members into individual landowners and farmers, encouraging their absorption into white society. This policy was advantageous to whites who were eager to acquire Indian land, but it proved disastrous for the Indians. One hundred thirty-eight million acres of reservation land were subdivided into tracts of 160, 80, or as little as 40 acres, and allotted tribe members on an individual basis. Land owned in this way was said to have "trust status" and could not be sold. But the surplus land—all Indian land not allotted to individuals—was opened (for sale) to white settlers. Ultimately, more than 90 million acres of land were taken from the Indians by legal and illegal means.

The resulting loss of land was a catastrophe for the Indians. It was necessary to make it illegal for Indians to sell their land to non-Indians. The Indian Reorganization Act of 1934 officially ended the allotment period. Tribes that voted to accept the provisions of this act were reorganized, and an effort was made to purchase land within preexisting reservations to restore an adequate land base.

Ten years later, in 1944, federal Indian policy again shifted. Now the federal government wanted to get out of the "Indian business." In 1953 an act of Congress named specific tribes whose trust status was to be ended "at the earliest possible time." This new law enabled the United States to end unilaterally, whether the Indians wished it or not, the special status that protected the land in Indian tribal reservations. In the 1950s federal Indian policy was to transfer federal responsibility and jurisdiction to state governments,

10

encourage the physical relocation of Indian peoples from reservations to urban areas, and hasten the termination, or extinction, of tribes.

Between 1954 and 1962 Congress passed specific laws authorizing the termination of more than 100 tribal groups. The stated purpose of the termination policy was to ensure the full and complete integration of Indians into American society. However, there is a less benign way to interpret this legislation. Even as termination was being discussed in Congress, 133 separate bills were introduced to permit the transfer of trust land ownership from Indians to non-Indians.

With the Johnson administration in the 1960s the federal government began to reject termination. In the 1970s yet another Indian policy emerged. Known as "self-determination," it favored keeping the protective role of the federal government while increasing tribal participation in, and control of, important areas of local government. In 1983 President Reagan, in a policy statement on Indian affairs, restated the unique "government is government" relationship of the United States with the Indians. However, federal programs since then have moved toward transferring Indian affairs to individual states, which have long desired to gain control of Indian land and resources.

As long as American Indians retain power, land, and resources that are coveted by the states and the federal government, there will continue to be a "clash of cultures," and the issues will be contested in the courts, Congress, the White House, and even in the international human rights community. To give all Americans a greater comprehension of the issues and conflicts involving American Indians today is a major goal of this series. These issues are not easily understood, nor can these conflicts be readily resolved. The study of North American Indian history and culture is a necessary and important step toward that comprehension. All Americans must learn the history of the relations between the Indians and the federal government, recognize the unique legal status of the Indians, and understand the heritage and cultures of the Indians of North America.

A Quechan woman collecting clay from the same area that her ancestors had visited for this purpose for centuries. The pot on her head, supported by a protective woven ring of cloth, will be used to carry the clay.

LIVING ALONG THE COLORADO

Kukumat was the creator of all people. He lived with one of the women he had made and she gave birth to a son, Kumastamxo. After his father's death, Kumastamxo led the people to a mountain called Avikwame. There he taught them how to cure illness; he also gave them bows and arrows. Kumastamxo then dismissed the people, who left Avikwame in groups. Each group traveled to a different area along a great river that Kumastamxo had created by tracing a course through the desert with the tip of his lance. One group journeyed south on a trail called *xam kwacan*, which means "another going down." They settled on fertile lands north of the river's mouth.

These people were the ancestors of the Quechan (pronounced kwuh TSAN) Indians, a tribe that still lives along the Colorado, the river Kumastamxo created, according to the Quechan's traditional account of their origins. Today they are often referred to as the Yuma, a name given them by Spaniards in the 16th century, but they prefer to be called the Quechan.) De-

rived from xam kwacan, this name recalls their ancient origins and reminds them of their deep roots in the Colorado valley.

The Colorado River used to be one of the most sediment-filled rivers in the world. Almost every spring, the river became swollen with the runoff of melting snow from the high plateau above it. Water overflowed its banks, carrying tons of rich soil over the low, broad valleys near the river's mouth in the Gulf of California. This annual flooding made these valleys extremely fertile, in contrast to the desert land that surrounded them. Where the floodplain ended, the vegetation was sparse and scraggly, and the low mountains nearby were huge, bare chunks of chocolate-colored rock that shimmered in the waves of intense summer heat. The terrain of sand hills just 60 miles north of the river's mouth was so barren that it stifled even the hardiest desert plant life.

Today the mighty Colorado has been tamed by dams. Much of its water is diverted for use on farms and in cities

today

13

before it can reach the gulf. As a result, the river's mouth has narrowed and its salt content has risen to dangerous levels. The Quechan now live on a reservation in southern California on the Colorado's west bank, directly across the river from the city of Yuma, Arizona. An interstate highway and a railroad run near each other through the reservation, but most travelers passing through are probably unaware that they are anywhere near an Indian community. The modern transportation route actually follows one that has been used by Indians for centuries and has long been known to non-Indians looking for the best way to travel west across the river into what is now California.

At Yuma the Colorado narrows to pass between two low, rocky hills; here it can be crossed easily when it is not flooded. The Quechan once controlled this area, now known as Yuma Crossing, as well as another vital area just to its north, the point where the Gila River joins the Colorado. The crossing, the river juncture, and the river itself all helped to shape the Quechan's history.

Despite the changes to the landscape, the Quechan today still recognize this region as their tribe's homeland. The peaks and other local

The Colorado River at Yuma Crossing as it appears today.

geographical features are described in the Quechan's ancient stories: They can see around them the area where a mourning party rested long ago or the place where Quechan went centuries before to collect a special kind of clay. Recalling such events affirms the Quechan's sense of their cultural heritage.

Just how long the Quechan have been in this area is not known, although archaeological research provides some information about the Indians who first lived in the Colorado valley. Archaeologists can learn about an ancient people from the artifacts—objects that people made, such as pottery or tools—that they left behind. The Colorado River has probably destroyed many artifacts over the centuries, but by studying those that have been unearthed, archaeologists believe that people were probably living in the region by the end of the last Ice Age in North America, in about 10,000 B.C. These people moved from place to place in small bands of probably fewer than 100 people, gathering wild plants as these ripened in various locales and hunting game. They lived in temporary camps, perhaps returning to the same spot for a particular season every year but never staying in one place for very long.

This way of life lasted for thousands of years. In about A.D. 500, the people in the Southwest began to make pottery and perhaps to grow crops in the river bottomlands. They probably learned the basic techniques of both activities from peoples east and west of them,

peoples with whom they came in contact along trade routes that stretched from what is now the Pacific coast to lands well to the east of the Colorado River.

At this time, the Indian groups living along the river near the present-day town of Parker, Arizona, participated in a trade network that was dominated by the complex Hohokam culture to their east. Like the Colorado River Indians, the Hohokam people grew crops, but the Hohokam also constructed vast networks of irrigation canals. These canals channeled the water of the Gila and Salt rivers into the Hohokam's desert fields and into their major population center, known today as Snaketown by archaeologists. The Hohokam themselves were influenced by the cultures that existed some 1,250 miles to the southeast. Archaeologists who have excavated Snaketown have found ball courts, low platform mounds, mirrors made from the mineral pyrite, and small bells that were cast from copper—all things that have also been found at sites far to the south in the Valley of Mexico.

For several centuries, the Hohokam people traded goods such as pottery and woven blankets for seashells and other items from the Pacific coast with Indians living west of the Colorado River. Archaeologists have found Hohokam pottery from Snaketown along the Colorado River and at its junction with the Gila River. Its presence there indicates that the Hohokam had continuing contact with the Colorado River

THE YUMAN LANGUAGE

The many different languages spoken by the world's people are grouped together into larger categories called "linguistic families." Membership in a linguistic family is based on similarities in pronunciation, syntax (word order), and spelling (for languages that have a written form). The different groups of people whose languages are in the same linguistic family do not necessarily live in the same geographic region or have identical ways of life. According to linguists, scholars who study the structure and evolution of languages, similarities among the languages of different groups indicate that at one time they did belong to a unified social group living in a particular region. The "parent" culture subdivided into smaller groups at various times in the past. As these smaller groups moved to different geographic regions, their languages, like their ways of life, continued to evolve in isolation from one another. Over long periods of time, this process brought about enough linguistic changes to give each group its own distinct language.

The language spoken by the Quechan is related to the languages of the Mohave, Maricopa, Cocopa, and Yavapai, among others. These languages all belong to the Yuman linguistic family. Their speakers live scattered through the southwestern United States.

The Quechan people did not have an alphabet to represent their language in writing. Linguists, however, have developed a way to represent Quechan words using the Roman alphabet and other symbols, known as diacritical marks, to indicate sounds of the Quechan language that do not occur in English.

Indian groups between A.D. 1050 and 1250.

But by 1050 some of these groups may have moved away from the river to the shores of a large inland sea, which was formed in about 900 and located west of the Colorado near what is now the Salton Sea in Imperial Valley,

California. The sea, known today as Lake Cahuilla, is long extinct; it existed for only a few hundred years, but this was long enough to attract several small Indian groups to its shores.

As the lake began to dry up, the Indians who had settled around it scattered in different directions. Perhaps

Vowels

a	as in father	kar?úk
e	as in met	Quechan
i	as in pin	xuksíl
o	as in hot	matxal cadóm
u	as in boot	xuksíl

Consonants

Most are pronounced as in English, with the following exceptions:

c	intermediate between **ts** and **ch**	xam kwacan
d	as in **this**	cadóm
r	not found in English; a rolled or trilled sound similar to the Spanish *r* as in *amor*	kar?úk
x	not found in English; similar to the Spanish *x* in Mexico or the German *ch* in *ich*	xam kwacan

The symbol *?* appearing in the middle of a word (kar?úk) indicates a glottal stop. This is the barely voiced sound, almost a catch in the throat, such as many people use when pronouncing the word *bottle* (bot?l).

An accent mark (´) indicates the stressed or emphasized syllable of the word unless the last syllable is stressed.

entire settlements or even small clusters of settlements moved back east to the banks of the Colorado. By 1150 to 1200 one of these settlements or settlement clusters had arrived at the river north of the Colorado-Gila junction. These people may have been the direct ancestors of the Quechan.

Although the members of the various Lake Cahuilla settlements traveled to the Colorado River separately, these groups soon formed alliances with other settlements. These alliances perhaps recreated those that had existed earlier when these peoples had all lived along the shores of the lake. As these

This shell, etched with an image of a horned toad, was excavated from a Hohokam site. Shells were among the goods the Hohokam traded to Indian groups to the east.

bonds became more formal and permanent, the allied settlements formed tribes, larger population groupings united by kinship, culture, and language. Among these tribes were the Quechan, the Mojave, and the Maricopa, whose descendants all speak languages that belong to the River Yuman branch of the Yuman linguistic family.

The stimulus for the formation of these tribal groups may well have been warfare, which increased as the tribes began to compete for control over east-west trade routes. By about 1200 the great Hohokam culture started to collapse, possibly because of crop failures or raids on their settlements by Indians

to the east. At this time some Yuman-speaking tribes moved eastward into land along the Gila River formerly occupied by the Hohokam people. The trade routes in this region were extremely important to these tribes. Not only would control of the routes probably have given a tribe wealth and power, it might also have ensured a constant food supply. The floods of the Colorado River usually provided an abundance of rich soil, but in some years there was little or no spring flooding or it came too late in the season and washed out newly planted fields. The Quechan and their neighbors then relied on gathering wild plants, such as pods of the mesquite tree, and fishing for their food. The occasional lack of crops may have led tribes to seek additional food by trading with Indian groups away from the river. Although foods from another region would have added variety to the Indians' diets, the amount that could be obtained through trade was probably limited. Therefore the groups most likely to have a secure food supply were those who controlled the trade routes.

The tribes along the Colorado River between 1200 and 1540 may also have clashed over access to fertile river bottomland. When the emigrants from Lake Cahuilla returned to the river, they must have encountered other groups who had never left the area north of the Colorado-Gila confluence. The clusters of former lakeside settlements may have become tribes after joining together as fighting units in an attempt to displace groups already living along the river. It is also possible that at first there was enough land for all the newcomers. But as their populations grew, the squabbles between the various groups over control of the best land may have escalated into warfare, which in turn led to the formation of tribes.

A tribe most likely developed from settlements that were geographically close to one another. The sense of unity among inhabitants of neighboring settlements was strong because the people sometimes intermarried and often gathered together for important ceremonies as well as informal social occasions. The tribal identity among the people along the Colorado and Gila rivers was unusually strong, which distinguished them from neighboring tribes.

In addition to information learned from archaeological data, we depend on early written descriptions for details about a tribe's culture or any people's way of life in the past. The first written records of the Quechan date from the 16th century, when Spaniards first arrived in their lands. Accounts of the "traditional" Quechan way of life written by early European explorers and settlers, however, are not completely reliable. The most informative were written between 1780 and 1860. By this time the Quechan had long been in contact with Europeans and Americans, whose efforts to "civilize" Indians by

A 19th-century engraving showing the waterline and shores of the extinct Lake Cahuilla.

teaching them the ways of white society had already altered or destroyed many of the tribe's traditions. The information that is available about the early history of the Quechan therefore may not provide an accurate picture of how they lived long ago.

When the Spanish began to explore the Colorado, there were perhaps 4,000 Quechan. About 1,000 died soon afterward, many from diseases such as measles and smallpox, which the Spaniards had brought with them from Europe. The Quechan population remained at about 3,000 until the mid-19th century, when it began another decline.

The Quechan produced approximately half of their food by farming. Their farming season and techniques were determined by the flooding pattern of the Colorado. Just before the spring floods, Quechan men would clear the brush from the fields at the river bottomlands. After the floodwaters had been absorbed by the earth and cracks began to appear in the rich silt (usually in late June or early July), entire families would move out to the fields to plant their crops. Men did the heavier work, such as digging the planting holes; women planted the seeds for the traditional Indian crops of corn, beans, and squash. By the late 16th century, the Quechan also began to grow wheat, black-eyed beans, watermelons, and muskmelons—European plants that the Spanish had introduced to North America. On less fertile land the tribespeople planted wild grasses and later

A six-inch-high ceramic Quechan vessel. Although its shape is similar to that of pots used by the Quechan to carry water, the vessel's small size and decoration suggests that it was made for sale or trade.

harvested the grass seed, which women ground and used to make cakes.

Although most of the Quechan's crops were planted in the late spring, the growing conditions of some plants permitted the Quechan to sow and harvest crops at other times of the year. Some corn and melons were planted in February and harvested in June; winter wheat was sown in the fall and reaped just before the spring floods.

The Quechan's crops did not demand much attention. The members of a household might weed their fields only once or twice during the growing season. Because there was little rainfall in the region, they may occasionally have had to haul water from the Col-

Quechan women stored crops in large baskets such as these on the roof of a 19th-century home.

orado River in small pots to irrigate their fields by hand, but the river floodwater retained by the soil usually provided enough moisture to sustain the crops. The Quechan did not need to add fertilizers to their fields because there was a wealth of minerals and nutrients already in the rich river silt.

The men, women, and older children of each household worked together to harvest crops after they had ripened. Often the Quechan would help their neighbors, making harvesttime a social occasion. Generally men brought the crops in from the fields and women stored them. Quechan women buried some of the harvest in storage pits on high ground. They also stored some in large woven baskets on small platforms built just above the ground or on the roofs of *ramadas*—flat-topped, open-walled, brush-covered sheds that

A Quechan woman grinding corn on a me-tate (grinding stone). A woman's ability to perform this labor quickly was so valued that a prospective bride had to demonstrate her grinding proficiency to her future mother-in-law before her marriage.

the Quechan built adjacent to their homes to shade the dwellings from the sun. These baskets looked like huge birds' nests and often measured four to six feet in diameter.

Despite the fertility of the river's silt, the Quechan were sometimes not able to grow and store enough crops to last from one harvest to the next. Food was typically most scarce in late May and June and in January and early February. At these times, the Quechan relied on hunting, fishing, and gathering wild plants to increase their food supply.

Quechan men hunted rabbits and birds in the early spring when there were few fish in the Colorado and when most of the plants the Quechan had gathered were not yet ripe. But usually there were few animals to hunt in the harsh desert terrain, so fish was the major source of animal protein in the Quechan's diet. A three-foot-long species of minnow and the humpback sucker were often plentiful in the Colorado River. To catch them, the Quechan used nets as well as hooks and lines. They also blocked streams with weirs, fences made of arrowweed that trapped fish so that they could easily be netted or grabbed.

The bean pods of the mesquite and screwbean trees were probably the most important wild food that the Quechan gathered. Sweet-tasting mesquite pods ripened in late June or early July, screwbeans about a month later. Women and children gathered them and turned their planting duties over to the men if necessary. Women dried the pods and ground them into meal or flour that they mixed with water to make cakes. They also allowed the pods to ferment in water to make a mildly intoxicating drink.

The Quechan regarded themselves as a single tribe, although they lived in several separate settlements rather than in one large village. Each settlement comprised several hundred people, each of whom also belonged to a household. A household usually contained members of an extended family: a group of related males, their wives and children, and often one or two more distant relatives or friends. A newly married couple most often would become part of the husband's household, but if his household already had too many mouths to feed or if the newlyweds were needed to work in the fields of the wife's family, the couple would move into the wife's household.

The Quechan moved in and out of households freely, but a married couple or a single person never lived alone. It would have been impossible for just one or two people living apart from other relatives to survive economically. Quechan households were practical social units: The river bottomlands could best be farmed successfully by a fairly large group of people working cooperatively in the fields.

Each household member had specific responsibilities. For instance, able-bodied adults and older children farmed and foraged, while the elders watched the youngsters. An especially close relationship consequently existed between grandparents and grandchildren in a household. Grandparents were teachers and disciplinarians as well as caretakers. Because of their knowledge and experience, elderly Quechan and their opinions were respected by all the members of the household.

Each household moved twice a year because of the Colorado River's annual cycle of flooding. In fall, winter, and early spring, the households escaped the river floodwaters by clustering together into settlements called *rancherias*, which were located on high ground away from the floodplain. There house-

A charm made of braided horsehair. The Quechan hung such ornaments around an infant's neck to help it grow strong.

A ramada (sun shade) next to a dome-shaped hut, photographed in the early 1900s.

holds built one or more dome-shaped shelters made from arrowweed. Every home had an open-sided ramada adjacent to it. In each rancheria there were one or two large houses that were covered on three sides with earth. The fourth wall was made of vertical posts that supported horizontal slats, between which the Quechan stuffed arrowweed for additional shelter. These spacious and durable homes were usually occupied by the households of the rancheria leaders, but if the weather became particularly cold they could shelter a large number of the rancheria's other inhabitants for a short time as well. These houses served as social centers for people living in the rancheria and their guests. The flat roofs of the buildings sometimes functioned as speaking platforms for the leaders.

When the floodwaters receded, the households moved to their farming plots in the bottomlands, where they stayed until after the fall harvest. There they lived in small arrowweed huts with adjoining ramadas, both of which they probably had to rebuild each year on the family's fields. Usually a household returned to the same fields every year unless one of its members had died. In such a case, the household would abandon its fields and move on to unoccupied ground elsewhere. The land would remain uncultivated until another household claimed it.

After the fall harvest, the households resettled upland in their rancheria homes. A rancheria would move from one site to another if the river changed course or if the inhabitants feared an enemy attack. Whenever the Quechan were forced to change the location of a rancheria, they looked for a new homesite that was high enough to escape the river's floods, but close enough to the river for them to easily move back to their farmlands when the floods receded. They also desired a location with some trees that could provide adequate wood for building materials and fuel.

Possibly the largest and most permanent of the Quechan rancherias was *Xuksíl* (Sandstone), which was located at the foot of a low mountain known now as Pilot Knob, just southwest of Yuma Crossing. In 1774, Spaniards estimated the population of Xuksíl as more than 800. Another major rancheria along the river about seven miles northeast of the crossing was *Matxal cadóm* (the North Group). At least two more were located north of the crossing; one of these, in what is now called the Palo Verde valley, was probably the northernmost Quechan settlement at that time. The Spanish found other Quechan rancherias scattered along the Gila River to the east for about 20 miles.

The members of a rancheria considered themselves to be relatives, which most of them probably were, either by blood or by marriage. They also believed themselves to be slightly superior to the inhabitants of the other Quechan settlements, even though all the Quechan belonged to the same tribe. Members of different rancherias probably spoke slightly different dialects or linguistic variations, which allowed the Quechan to identify which rancheria a person came from by his or her speech.

The hill known as Pilot Knob. Xuksíl, the largest of the Quechan's ancient settlements, was established at its foot.

The various rancherias came together for funerals and mourning rituals and for harvest ceremonies in the fall, and their warriors joined forces in major war expeditions. But the rancherias probably also squabbled with one another from time to time. For instance, members of one might take offense at something the inhabitants of another rancheria did, or the leaders of different rancherias might disagree about such matters as when to launch a war party or how best to deal with outsiders.

Each Quechan also belonged to a clan. The clans may have originated in the small settlements that had existed centuries earlier, before the Quechan developed a tribal identity. Members of each clan were scattered throughout the rancherias by 1780, but some rancherias included most of the individuals belonging to certain clans. For example, most members of the *Xipá panyá* clan lived in a rancheria that was known as Sunflowerseed Eaters in the late 1800s.

Clans were patrilineal; their membership was traced in the male line and therefore children belonged to the clan of their father. At one time clan membership may have dictated a Quechan's duties in the tribe's mourning ritual, but over the years this and other clan functions lost most of their significance. By the late 19th century the clans' primary purpose was to regulate the selection of marriage partners. A man and woman of the same clan could not marry each other; the relationship was "too close," according to the Quechan. They believed that the children produced by such a union would "never turn out right."

Each clan had a totem, or symbol, associated with it. Typically a clan totem was an animal, such as a red ant, a frog, a snake, or a buzzard, but some

Seven ears of prehistoric corn discovered in 1941 near the Quechan's homeland. Corn was one of the tribe's most important crops and the totem of several different clans.

clans had corn as their totem. The Quechan had a special feeling for their clan totems, but unlike many tribes the Quechan did not have any myths or rituals involving the totems. Most Quechan regarded their totem merely as the name of their clan, although they might attribute the character trait of an individual to his or her totem. For instance, a Quechan might say, "You notice how that man is so cross all the time? Well, what else can you expect? His totem is a snake."

Quechan boys and girls underwent special ceremonies to mark their transition from childhood to young adulthood. In many other Indian cultures, such ceremonies taught young adolescents about clan lore and rituals. But because clans were relatively unimportant to the Quechan, their ceremonies instructed boys and girls about what their roles as men and women of the tribe would be. These initiation rituals were physically and mentally demanding ordeals. But because the experiences were so grueling, neither they nor the lessons the rituals impressed upon young Quechan were easily forgotten.

When a Quechan boy was between 8 and 10 years old, he, along with a small group of other boys his age, went through a 4-day ritual to test his endurance. On the first day, the soft flesh between each boy's nostrils was pierced by an adult male, who put a string through the hole to keep the wound open. Then, under the watchful eyes of

An adult Quechan man wearing a nose ring. Traditionally, all boys had their noses pierced during a grueling initiation rite.

these men, the boys ran in the heat of the sun for 10 or 15 miles to the north. On the second day, they ran the same distance to the west; on the third day, to the south; and on the fourth day, to the east. The men who supervised the ordeal kept the boys up at night, constantly grilling them with questions, and gave them only watery corn mush to eat. On the fourth day, the men removed the strings from the boys' noses and replaced them with short grease-wood sticks, which the boys wore until the hole had healed. As adults they would hang decorative beads and shells from these holes, as well as from holes in their earlobes. Although boys were not considered to be fully adult until their middle teens, they learned through this ceremony the importance of developing their physical endurance and other athletic skills so that they could become good warriors. The ordeal may also have created a special bond between the boys who went through it together, a camaraderie much like that of athletic teams today.

A girl's initiation ritual took place when she had her first menstrual period. Unlike a boy's ceremony, a girl's was a private family affair. Each day of the four-day ritual the girl lay on her stomach in a shallow pit. The pit was lined with stones that had been heated in a fire and covered with a layer of arrowweed. The warmth generated by this lining was believed to help the girl grow tall and straight. Then for several hours she was either buried in warm sand or wrapped in a warm blanket with only her head uncovered to allow her to breathe. At this time, the women of her household and their female guests sang songs and lectured her on how to behave as an ideal Quechan woman. At the end of each day, the girl was taken from the pit and washed. Throughout the ceremony, she was given little to eat and no meat or salt. She was also told not to touch her body

with her hands during the entire four days because if she did she would get black marks on her face and her hair would fall out. The girl was given a special stick to use if she needed to scratch herself. All Quechan women stayed in an isolation hut apart from other people when they were menstruating. During this time they touched their body only with a stick and avoided meat and salt.

The girl's initiation ceremony impressed upon her the bonds of cooperation and support that united the family. Only after a girl had gone

Bows, arrows, feather headdresses, a rattle, and a club used in the kar?úk mourning ceremony.

through this ritual could she be promised in marriage. Her parents and the parents of her future husband would arrange the marriage; she probably had little say in the choice of her mate. Her husband would generally be several years older than she and might already have one or more wives.

A Quechan marriage linked not only two individuals, but also the two households from which they came. A wife's ties to her husband's household remained strong even if her husband died. When this happened, one of the husband's brothers would be expected to offer to marry the widow to demonstrate that his household continued to care about her. The widow, however, did not have to accept the proposal.

The Quechan also performed rituals whenever a member of the tribe died. At funeral ceremonies, they cremated the corpse and destroyed the deceased's house and personal belongings. The rubble at the site of the cremation and where the house once stood was then smoothed over, so as to leave no physical traces of the deceased's existence. After the funeral, the name of the deceased no longer was mentioned and the household's farmlands were abandoned. The Quechan wanted to destroy all reminders of the dead because, as they explained, the memory made them sad.

There was at least one time during the year when the memories of the dead did come flooding back. This was during the mourning ceremony called the kar?úk, which commemorated the death of gifted leaders or brave warriors. It was also meant to give the people strength and ease the sorrow of those who had recently lost a family member. The kar?úk was traditionally held at irregular intervals, but by the end of the 19th century it had virtually become an annual ritual.

Major ceremonies in most cultures serve to remind the participants of what their people consider truly important. The kar?úk ritual emphasized two themes. First, it reenacted the cremation ritual described in the Quechan's ancient story of the mourning ceremony that followed the death of their creator Kukumat. In this way the kar?úk reminded the people of their origins and symbolized their common heritage. Second, the ritual featured a mock battle; this made the Quechan recall the vital role of warfare in their lives.

Each Quechan settlement had a leader called a *pa?ipá ta?axán* (real man). Usually this position was passed from father to son, but the people would support the most competent male leader regardless of his family line. This leader was always one of the wisest men in the settlement. He had to be the best speaker as well because every morning he addressed the people, giving them news and offering a few well-chosen words of encouragement for the coming day's activities. The Quechan also wanted their leader to be kind, generous to the poor, and always willing to put the interests of the people above his own.

The Quechan believed that these leadership qualities came from a special power that certain people received through dreams. Everyone dreamed, of course. But not everyone dreamed the special power-bestowing dreams. These Quechan were transported in their sleep to Avikwame or another mountain or high plateau, where they were told by spirits how to behave. They usually related such dreams to a group of elderly religious leaders who would interpret the dreams' significance. These elders then watched the dreamers closely to determine whether their behavior or character showed that a dream had truly been powerful. If so, the dreamer could one day become a leader.

Dream power was a requirement for most of the honored positions in Quechan life. But dreams only signaled the potential for greatness; a person also had to learn and master certain necessary skills to perform any important role. For instance, a warrior needed both dream power and the ability to use a club, a spear, and a bow and arrow.

Dream power helped Quechan curers determine the cause of an illness, but they had to learn various techniques to treat it. A common cure for several different illnesses was to blow tobacco smoke and spray saliva over the patient and then massage the person's body. Quechan curers usually specialized in treating only one ailment, such as snakebites, broken bones, or arrow wounds. Some could cure several, but no curer could treat every disorder.

The Quechan did not think that an illness or injury occurred by accident. They believed that all ailments were caused by persons with special powers who for some reason wanted to harm their victims. Europeans and Americans referred to such people as "witches," implying they were evil. Yet those Quechan who had the power to cause harm also had the power to get rid of it. Whether one of these powerful individuals was an evil witch or a kindly curer thus depended on the patient's point of view.

The Quechan with the greatest dream power was the *kwaxót*, the religious leader of the entire tribe. He presided over all the tribal rituals and contacted supernatural beings when the Quechan needed their help. For instance, the kwaxót might ask these spirits to bring rain if the Quechan's fields were dry or to create a dust storm to confuse an enemy war party. He also was expected to make fine speeches and always be kind and even-tempered. Like the settlement leaders, the kwaxót held his position only for as long as he had the support of the people; therefore, he could not be a tyrant who imposed his will on those he represented. All important decisions of tribal and settlement life were made by consensus, after much discussion among household heads, rancheria leaders, and the kwaxót.

A rattle crafted by Robert Escalante in 1982 from a gourd, cottonwood, clay, pebbles, and enamel paint. Gourd rattles tradition-ally were used at Quechan ceremonies and by curers.

The responsibility for planning and supervising Quechan war parties belonged to leaders known as *kwanamí*. In the 18th and 19th centuries, Europeans and Americans often tried to single out one of these men as *the* tribal war chief. But any Quechan man who showed unusual bravery and aggressiveness in combat could become a kwanamí, and sometimes there were several living in one rancheria at the same time. The Quechan also honored a woman who showed an unusual talent for fighting against enemies by conferring a special title on her.

Warfare was a tribal passion. In addition to fighting to control trade and good river bottomland, the Quechan continually battled the other tribes along the Colorado to take captives (usually women and children), whom they either incorporated into the tribe or traded as slaves for horses or other goods. But for the Quechan, war was also a way to strengthen the tribe's spiritual power and at the same time demonstrate it to others. This power came in part from taking the scalps of dead and wounded enemies.

The Quechan took scalps only after they had won a battle, because the victors always controlled the battlefield after a clash. The warriors of a defeated tribe could not take scalps in retaliation, but they did try to drag away as many of their own casualties as possible before the victors descended on them. Because scalps were powerful and had to be handled carefully lest they bring misfortune to the tribe, only a Quechan with dream power could scalp the enemy. A scalper first broke a fallen enemy warrior's neck across his knee. Using a knife, he would cut the flesh across the bridge of the nose, across the cheeks under the eyes, below the ears, and around to the back of the neck, from where he then pulled off the scalp. A short ritual was performed on the battleground to celebrate the scalpings, and another was held in the rancheria when the war party returned. The kwaxót was the keeper of the scalps, which were sealed in pots and buried.

If Quechan scalps were taken by an enemy, the tribe's warriors usually made a retaliatory raid to avenge the victims. Quechan warriors also fre-

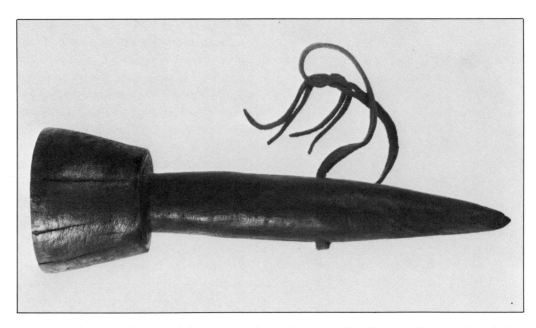

A 7½-inch-long wooden war club with a leather wrist strap. Quechan warriors attacked their enemies in hand-to-hand combat by first ramming the club's pointed end into their opponents' stomach and then using the weapon's broad head to bludgeon them in the face.

quently launched small raids on other tribes merely to stir up mischief and perhaps to take a few captives before the enemy could muster a large defensive force. Major expeditions were more carefully planned and may have involved more than 100 warriors.

When Quechan forces arrived in enemy territory, they assembled in battle lines and waited as the enemy warriors formed similar lines facing them. Several kwanamí exchanged shouted insults with the enemy leaders. The leaders of both tribes then began to fight and were soon joined by their warriors.

Quechan warriors used several types of weapons. When the enemy was a distance away, the Quechan shot at them with wooden arrows launched by bows. The arrows were not usually tipped with stone or metal heads, but the Quechan carved one end of each arrow to a point so sharp that it could penetrate the body of an enemy warrior and kill him. In hand-to-hand combat, the Quechan attacked opponents with clubs made from the wood of a mesquite tree and with flint knives that they carried clenched in their teeth. Some men also carried wooden spears. After they learned to ride horses, which were brought to North America by the Spanish, some Quechan warriors rode into battle armed with lances. On major military expeditions, a rank of Quechan women used short wooden staffs to kill the enemy's wounded.

The Quechan were usually the allies of the Mojave, who lived to the north along the Colorado River. Their primary enemies were the Maricopa and the Cocopa, who according to early Spanish explorers also lived on the banks of the Colorado at the beginning of the 17th century. By the late 1600s, however, the combined Quechan-Mojave forces had driven the Maricopa eastward to the banks of the Gila River.

They eventually also pushed other Colorado River tribes, including the Kavelchadom, Kahwan, Halyikwamai, and Halchidhoma, into the Maricopa's new territory. This warfare not only brought the tribe spiritual power, but also gave the Quechan control of the most vital resource in the region: the Colorado River. The battle to maintain this control brought the Quechan into conflict with Spaniards and Americans, who would be among their most formidable enemies. ▲

Christian Indian laborers at a mission in Alta California. The Indians and missionaries are assembled to welcome a group of French scholars that visited the region in the late 18th century.

2

SOLDIERS, PRIESTS, AND COLONIAL INTRIGUE

The Spanish were drawn to North America in the 16th century by the lure of two kinds of riches: precious metals (principally gold and silver) and land (for agriculture and settlement). In the name of the king of Spain, *conquistadores* (conquerors) battled the Indian groups who originally owned the minerals and land they desired and then shared their plunder with the crown. The Indians also provided a third resource that the Spanish needed in order to realize fully their colonial aims—laborers. Only human labor could extract the land's riches. After they were conquered, the Indians were forced to work the fields and mines that were taken from them by the Spanish.

After the Spanish decided that Indians were in fact human beings (early conquistadores had some doubts about this), the crown felt obligated to "civilize" those who performed labor for them. Catholic priests began to accompany the conquistadores into the Indians' lands and sought converts there as

eagerly as the soldiers sought gold. These missionaries destroyed most of the Indians' rich cultural heritage and replaced it with a mixture of Spanish and Roman Catholic traditions. The priests also snatched up many Indians who had avoided working in Spanish mines or fields and set them to work in Spanish missions.

Even though the Spanish needed Indian labor and acknowledged that Indians had souls to save, conquistadores and Spanish settlers managed to kill an appalling number of Indians. Thousands died in battle or from hard labor, but even more were felled by the diseases, such as measles and smallpox, that the Spaniards brought with them from Europe. These diseases spread quickly through Indian groups and devastated entire populations because, unlike the Spaniards, the Indians had no immunity to them.

The Spanish conquest of North America began in 1517 in what is today central Mexico. Conquistadores grad-

A 17th-century drawing showing the equipment carried by cavalrymen in New Spain. Each soldier's gear included a lance, a musket, pistols, a shield, and a cuera, *a leather coat that could not be penetrated by arrows.*

ually explored regions to the north, but it was not until 1540 that Spaniards arrived in the area of the confluence of the Colorado and Gila rivers. Hernando de Alarcón and a small group of soldiers were the first Spaniards to travel up the Colorado by boat. They were part of a large expedition led by Francisco Vásquez de Coronado that had been sent northward from Mexico City to explore what is now the southwestern United States. Coronado and his men had heard rumors that the Indians along the Colorado had fabulous stores of gold and other precious goods, and he sent Alarcón to find a possible water route to the area. Alarcón may have reached Yuma Crossing before turning back downriver. Several weeks after Alarcón's expedition, another detachment of Coronado's men, headed by Melchior Díaz, reached the crossing by traveling overland. Neither group stayed long, although the Spaniards did talk with the Indians there through Indian interpreters they had brought with them, and they left the Indians a few Spanish trinkets.

The Quechan at that time were living north of the confluence and may have had no direct contact with the Spaniards at the time of either expedition. But they certainly must have heard about the visits of the strange white men, about their gifts, and especially about their awesome guns.

Sixty-three years would pass before the Quechan themselves are known to have encountered Spaniards. In 1603 Juan de Oñate, 30 soldiers, and 2 priests arrived in a Quechan rancheria about 100 miles north of the Colorado-Gila confluence and Yuma Crossing. The inhabitants welcomed the newcomers. The kwaxót invited the Spaniards to stay, but they traveled instead to another rancheria downriver. The Quechan there told Oñate that they traded with tribes to the west and with Indians who lived on an island off the Pacific coast. Oñate left some cotton blankets for the Quechan to trade to the islanders for precious metals and shells that Oñate planned to pick up on his return journey. The Quechan then furnished guides for the Spaniards' trip south to the Colorado's mouth. When Oñate and his men returned early in 1605 the

An inscription carved into a rock near Quechan territory in 1606 by a member of Spaniard Juan de Oñate's expedition to explore the region of the Colorado and Gila rivers. The message reads, "I passed through here in advance of Juan de Oñate in search of the sea of the south [the Gulf of California]."

Quechan gave him the white shell beads for which they had traded his blankets. They also staged welcoming ceremonies for the Spaniards, in which Quechan warriors flung their bows and arrows to the ground in a symbolic gesture of friendship.

For the next century, the Quechan had little contact with the Spaniards, although they continued to hear of them from tribes living in the colonial province of Sonora, which the Spanish had established southeast of the Quechan homeland. During this time the tribe moved south along the Colorado River and took control of the Colorado-Gila confluence and Yuma Crossing, as well as more than 20 miles of land to the east along the Gila River. They displaced tribes that had been living in the area, such as the Maricopa and the Kavelchadom. Because these tribes were enemies of the Quechan during the 17th century, the Quechan and their Mojave allies probably drove them away from the Colorado by force.

In 1699 Father Eusebio Kino, a priest of the Jesuit order, visited several Quechan rancherias along the Gila River and at the confluence as he searched for a land route to link Sonora with the Jesuit missions that he had established in Baja California, in what is today Mexico. The Quechan welcomed Kino and gave his party, as he later wrote, "great quantities of fish, both cooked and raw" because the Indians' crops were not yet ripe. Wanting to stay on good terms with the Quechan leaders, Kino gave three of them ceremonial staffs as recognition of their leadership and handed out trinkets to the people. In November 1701 he also arranged to supply food to the Quechan. The Colorado River had not flooded the Quechan's best farmland that spring and consequently the crops had failed. Kino persuaded the Halyikwamai to the south to trade their excess crops to the Quechan even though the two tribes were enemies. Throughout the 18th century, Spaniards arranged intermittent peace agreements between the two tribes because they did not want warfare to endanger their access to the travel routes between Sonora and Baja California.

The Quechan were fond of Kino or at least of his gifts. Several times between 1701 and 1706 they sent Kino gifts of their own and messages asking him to return to their lands. Before Kino's last visit to the Quechan in 1706, the priest had introduced several goods that soon became important to the tribe, including Spanish wheat, horses, and other livestock. Kino's direct contact with the Quechan, however, was probably too brief for him to acquaint them with many of the traditions of Spanish Catholicism.

In the early 1700s, the Spanish began to deal with the Quechan more frequently, primarily because they needed to establish a land route to Baja California through Quechan territory. The Spanish also wanted to build forts along the Colorado River to keep other European nations, especially France, from establishing settlements in the region. The difficulty of traveling across the lower Colorado River at any point other than Yuma Crossing was thus both a curse and a blessing to Spanish colonial interests. From either point of view, control of the crossing was vital to the Spanish.

During the first half of the 18th century, the Spanish made little effort to take direct control of Yuma Crossing because their soldiers were occupied with suppressing Indian revolts throughout Sonora. The Pima, Papago, Apache, and other tribes frequently attacked Spanish settlements, destroyed or took their crops, and stole their horses and other livestock. Spanish military forces would storm into one region and subdue the Indian groups there temporarily, but soon they would be called away to squelch a revolt in another trouble spot. The Spanish did not have enough soldiers or money to create a fort, mission, or settlement at Yuma Crossing or anywhere else along the Colorado until the late 1700s.

San Xavier del Bac, photographed in 1908 by Edward Curtis. This was one of several missions established by Father Eusebio Kino in the Colorado River region in the early 1700s.

The Spaniards' harsh treatment of Indians inspired these revolts. It also led to more intensive fighting among the tribes themselves. Traditionally, Indians had taken captives during intertribal warfare. Now the Spanish, who became increasingly active in slave trading throughout the 18th century, were eager to buy Indians taken captive by any tribe. Some Indian groups, particularly the Apache, would stage raids against their enemies in order to grab a few captives to sell or trade to the Spaniards for horses and other goods. The Quechan sold war captives—probably through Pima or Papago intermediaries—and some Quechan were taken prisoner by other tribes and sold.

Throughout the turmoil of this period, the Quechan remained friendly to the Spanish and occasionally sent messages inviting Spaniards to visit them in the hope that they would bring gifts to the tribe. Jacobo Sedelmayr, a Jesuit priest who came to their lands in 1748, noted that the Quechan paid a great deal of attention to his party's horses, weapons, and other equipment.

By the early 1770s, there were fewer Indian revolts in Sonora, which freed the Spanish to establish a struggling new colony, Alta California, in what is now the state of California. Needing to ensure access to the land route between this colony and Sonora, the Spanish finally moved to gain control of Yuma Crossing and the Quechan who lived there. In 1771 Francisco Garcés, a Franciscan priest, visited the Quechan in order to scout a good route to Alta California and also to try to create peace among the various river tribes. But the Quechan, as usual, were most interested in the Spaniards' possessions. Juan Bautista de Anza, a captain in Garcés's party, wrote that the Quechan begged Garcés "to show them the compass, the glass for making fire, and other instruments which we [Spaniards] use." Garcés stayed briefly with the Quechan and then traveled northwest into Alta California, journeying overland almost to the ocean before turning back.

In 1774 and 1776, Captain Anza and Father Garcés again launched expeditions across the Colorado River and into Alta California. On these journeys they visited the Quechan and distributed gifts to them. The kwaxót Olleyquotequiebe (Wheezy One), whom the Spanish had named Salvador Palma, was particularly friendly after Captain Anza ceremoniously appointed him "governor" of the Quechan and gave him a red sash and a Spanish coin as symbols of this office. Keeping Palma as their ally was part of the Spaniards' plan to dominate the Colorado River region. Anza wrote, "With the present captain of the Yumas [Palma], if we know how to manage him, I think it will be possible to subdue the nearby tribes." Anza later presented Palma with a magnificent Spanish suit with a yellow-fronted jacket, a blue cape trimmed with gold braid, and a black velvet cap decorated with imitation jewels.

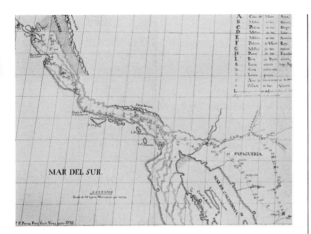

A map drawn by Father Pedro Font in 1776 showing the route of Captain Juan Bautista de Anza's expedition from Sonora to Alta California two years earlier.

An incident that occurred during the 1776 expedition suggested to the Spaniards that controlling the Quechan would not be simple. Father Pedro Font, one of the priests on the expedition, became irritated with the Indians' curiosity about his belongings. To get some privacy, he grabbed a long pole and dispersed the Quechan with it. One Quechan took great offense, and Font later reflected on the confrontation: "All their affability, which is more due to the gifts of beads than to their gentleness, might easily be converted to arrogance whenever an attempt is made to reduce them to the catechism and obedience."

Still, Salvador Palma remained friendly. In 1776 Anza took him, his brother Ygnacio Palma, and two other Indians (one perhaps was Pedro, the son of Pablo, leader of the Xuksíl rancheria) to Mexico City, which was the capital of Spain's colonies in North America (named New Spain). There the Indians were entertained, baptized into the Catholic church, and constantly reminded by Anza of Spain's interest in controlling Yuma Crossing. Palma declared that he would welcome Spanish missions among his people. In return, he hoped the Spanish would give them weapons to defend themselves against their Indian enemies. Palma and the others returned to the Quechan several months later, apparently convinced that the Spanish would soon come back to the crossing and shower the Quechan with goods. Rumors of these fabulous gifts quickly spread through the rancherias.

During their several extended visits between 1771 and 1776, the Franciscan priests had begun to attack traditional Quechan ways, particularly their marriage and curing practices. The priests insisted that an Indian man should have only one wife, and they mocked curers, whom they called "humbugs," and dream power. Palma reportedly responded by giving up all but one of his several wives and declaring himself eager for other Quechan men to do the same. Pablo, the powerful leader of Xuksíl, however, resisted. He and other Quechan had begun to dislike and distrust the Spaniards, especially after their horses and other livestock destroyed the Indians' wheat crop in January 1776. Despite these growing anti-Spanish feelings, the priests reported that some members of the tribe had learned to sing psalms and that many attended Catholic mass.

Early in 1777 King Philip II of Spain decreed that missionaries and soldiers would be sent to Quechan territory to establish a permanent station in order to secure Spain's claim to the area. He ordered that these Spaniards were to treat the Quechan with special care. The Indians' lands were not to be confiscated and their own leaders were to be kept in power. The king probably made this unusually respectful demand because he knew that Anza and others feared that if the Quechan were treated as brutally as other tribes in New Spain, the Spanish would not be able to gain control of Yuma Crossing.

The king's orders took time to carry out. Meanwhile, Palma became worried as his people grew restless wondering whether the Spaniards would ever arrive with gifts. Palma's leadership was in danger if they did not come soon. He visited Spanish authorities in Sonora in May 1777, March 1778, and early 1779 to ask that they send missionaries immediately. The Spanish finally sent Father Garcés to the region in August 1779 to keep the Quechan calm until the settlers could arrive.

Reporting that the tribe seemed less friendly than it had been earlier, Garcés urgently requested Spanish commander Teodoro de Croix to send him a supply of trade goods to appease the Quechan. Instead, in October, Croix sent another priest and a dozen soldiers, who brought scarcely enough goods to trade for their own food. The soldiers were met by Quechan clamoring for the gifts promised to Palma during his stay in Mexico City. The soldiers told the Indians that if they wanted goods, they would have to work for them. In November the Quechan angrily stripped Palma of his leadership and replaced him with his brother Ygnacio Palma. The Spaniards, however, remained loyal to Salvador Palma and continued to treat him as the leader of his rancheria.

The Quechan managed to live with this small number of Spaniards for another year, but the relationship between the two groups was extremely tense. Father Garcés reported that the Indians were not very receptive to Catholic teachings and continually requested more supplies, which were never sent. In October 1780, a few more soldiers and an unknown number of settlers arrived among the Quechan. This group came with practically no supplies of their own and expected to be given food from the Quechan's harvest until they could plant and harvest their own crops. But that year the Colorado River had failed to flood the best Quechan farmland; the harvest had been so poor that the Quechan did not have enough food for themselves.

To obtain more food the Quechan, led by Ygnacio Palma, went south to attack the Kahwans, whose harvest had been good. They killed or captured some Kahwans, burned many of their houses, and carried away as much food as they could. Fearing that Ygnacio Palma could also incite the Quechan to battle the Spanish, the priests sent messages to Sonora asking that Ygnacio be separated from his people. They also requested that no more settlers be allowed to come to the region until the following spring.

The Spanish authorities ignored the priests' pleas and soon sent more settlers to the confluence area. A large party of about 160 Spaniards, including 21 soldiers and about 107 women and

A 19th-century engraving depicting the forced conversion of Indians during the late 1700s. Despite Father Francisco Garcés's efforts, most Quechan rejected Catholic teachings.

children, arrived in late December 1780. They, too, brought practically no supplies with them, which placed an even greater strain on the Quechan's small store of food. The Spaniards' commander, Santiago Yslas, nonetheless reported that the Quechan received his party joyously.

The Spanish newcomers set to work creating two small settlements. One was on top of the rocky hill on the west bank of Yuma Crossing, which later became known as Fort Yuma Hill or Indian Hill. The other was about 10 or 12 miles farther downriver in the vicinity of the Xuksíl rancheria. Despite their industry, the settlers neglected some important tasks—building irrigation ditches and preparing their fields for spring planting.

By May 1781, the relationship between the Quechan and the Spaniards had grown more strained. Food was again scarce among the settlers because they had planted no crops. The Indians at Xuksíl objected to the settlers taking control of farmland near the rancheria. The Quechan had also resumed their warfare against neighboring tribes in spite of Spanish efforts to keep the peace. Father Garcés, angry because the Quechan continued to resist the teachings of Roman Catholicism, now wrote that they were "the most crude people on this frontier, and much too stupid to be attracted to spiritual things."

Although Ygnacio Palma had not been overly friendly to the Spanish, in late 1780 they nonetheless had given their official support and staffs of office to Ygnacio and to Pedro and declared them the leaders of the Xuksíl rancheria. (Pedro was a son of the former leader, Pablo, who had died some time earlier.) This ploy had seemed to win the two Quechan over to the Spanish cause. But at the end of May 1781, Commander Yslas arrested both Ygnacio and Pedro and locked them in stocks. It is not clear whether their crime had involved being rude to Father Garcés or plotting to kill a soldier. In making these arrests, Yslas had ignored the orders of the Spanish king and a later reminder from the commander's superiors in Sonora that the Quechan were to be treated with "much sweetness." The Quechan raised such an outcry that Yslas finally released his prisoners, but the public insult was not forgotten by the two leaders.

Salvador Palma had also grown angry at the Spaniards. Some months earlier, Yslas had erected a public whipping post and ordered Palma to whip Quechans who the commander believed were guilty of offenses against the Spanish. Palma obeyed promptly, but probably resented the order because Yslas had forced him to disregard the responsibility of any kwaxót (even a former one) to be kind and generous to his people. Palma was further upset in late May when the Spanish did not give him a new suit as they had promised. On this occasion Yslas arrogantly retorted that if Palma wanted Spanish clothes he would have to earn them.

Yet another Spanish expedition bound for California arrived at Yuma Crossing in early June 1781. As usual the Spaniards brought little food and few other supplies except livestock. Most of the expedition left the crossing about two weeks later, but they left behind 257 animals and about a dozen soldiers commanded by Fernando Rivera y Moncada, who allowed the livestock to trample and eat the crops in the Quechan's fields on the east side of the river. When Rivera's soldiers began molesting Quechan women, and the tribe learned from the Spaniards' Indian interpreters that Rivera wanted to kill the Indians, the Quechan wanted no more of Spanish colonialism.

Early in the morning of July 17, two groups of Quechan warriors launched surprise attacks against the Spanish settlements. Salvador Palma, Ygnacio Palma, Pedro, and two Indian interpreters led the Quechan forces. They destroyed the Spaniards' settlements and killed or captured all of the inhabitants. According to a Spanish account, Salvador Palma wanted to spare them, but Father Garcés and three other priests were murdered. By the afternoon of the following day, the Quechan had killed Rivera and his soldiers on the east side of the crossing as well. When the bloodshed had ended, 55 male settlers were dead and at least 76 Spaniards—most of them women and children—had been taken captive.

The Spanish retaliated in October 1781. They sent 90 soldiers under Lieutenant Colonel Pedro Fages to rescue the prisoners and capture and execute the Quechan leaders. When Fages's forces arrived, Salvador Palma, who was again the Quechan's kwaxót, returned many of the Spanish captives. The Spaniards themselves then took some Quechan prisoners, but although they tried to trap the Indians with promises of friendship, they never captured the tribal leaders.

From October 1871 to October 1872, Fages and other Spanish military commanders periodically battled the Quechan. During this time, the Spanish entered into an alliance with the Halchidhoma to the north. The Halchidhoma hoped that by joining with the Spanish forces they could overwhelm the Quechan and end the Quechan's steady raids against Halchidhoma settlements. Instead the alliance merely angered the Quechan, who with the Mojave eventually drove the Halchidhoma permanently up the Gila River to the east.

The statue of Father Francisco Garcés on the grounds of the Catholic mission that now stands on Indian Hill. Today many Quechan resent this monument to the priest who, in their view, oppressed their ancestors.

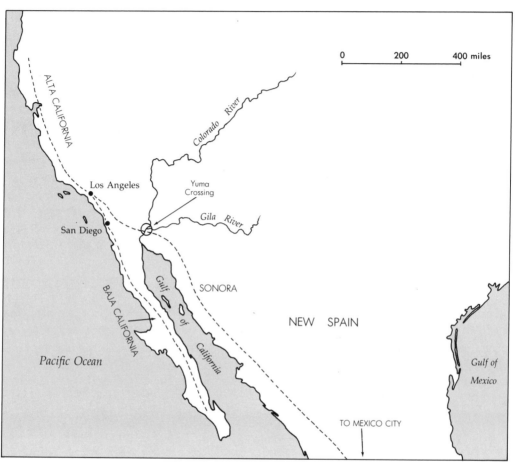

The Spanish also failed to defeat the Quechan. Spain never reestablished control of Yuma Crossing and therefore was not able to give proper support to its outposts in Alta California. Neither settlers nor supplies could easily move overland to or from San Diego or other settlements near the Spanish mission.

Eighty years of gift giving and short visits had created staunch Spanish allies among the Quechan; yet it took less than two years of close daily contact with Spaniards to change the Quechan into their bitter enemies. Compared to tribes living to their south and east, the Quechan were fortunate to suffer the direct effects of Spanish colonialism for only a short time. The populations of some Indian groups in Mexico, for instance, were devastated by warfare and European diseases. But between 1604 and 1800 the Quechan population dropped only about 25 percent, to about 3,000 people. Although some

Quechan were captured and sold as slaves, as a group they were never forced to work in Spanish mines or fields. They were not evicted from their territory and never had to live in Spanish-dominated settlements.

The Quechan's experience with the Spanish might have been different if the settlers and soldiers had followed the orders of their own officials. But the Spaniards at Yuma Crossing were convinced that they had to control the region's original residents and that to do so they had to control the Quechan leaders. When gifts and Catholic doctrine did not win them over, the Spaniards brought out chains and the whipping post to punish "bad" leaders and make an example of them for the other tribespeople. But the Spanish never had enough military strength at the crossing to prevent the Quechan from retaliating.

Spanish colonialism had its greatest impact upon the Quechan by making the tribespeople desire certain trade goods. During the years that Spaniards were in the region, trading relations among all tribes along the Colorado River changed as each tried to control trade with the Spanish. The Spaniards' eagerness to trade goods for slaves helped to increase warfare and threw the region into even greater turmoil than it had been in before. The Quechan adjusted by keeping themselves strong militarily and maintaining a close alliance with the equally strong Mojave to the north.

The Spanish, however, had little success in imposing their religion on the Quechan. Before 1781 some Quechan appeared to accept the Spaniards' Roman Catholicism, but probably only because they hoped to receive more Spanish gifts. After the 1781 revolt, however, even Salvador Palma, the staunchest Quechan convert to Catholicism, was rumored to have destroyed church images and lesson books in a renunciation of the faith.

Spanish ideals and principles— what the Spaniards were pleased to call "civilization"—seemed to have had even less impact on the tribe. The Quechan simply had no use for them, for in many ways they were already more civilized than the Spaniards. ▲

Principal Chief Pasqual standing between Yuma store owner and ferry operator L. J. F. Jaeger and Mrs. Jaeger in an 1870s photograph. Behind them are two unidentified Quechan men.

WHO CONTROLS
THE QUECHAN?

From 1781 until 1852 the Quechan again controlled Yuma Crossing. At different times during this period, Spaniards, Mexicans, and Americans all claimed that the Quechan's homeland belonged to them. But without unimpeded access to the crossing, none of these groups' claims gave them actual control over the region.

For years after the Quechan's 1781 revolt, the tribe was a barrier to overland trade between Spaniards in San Diego and those in settlements to the east of the Colorado River. The Spanish were further irritated to learn that the Quechan and their Mojave allies were sheltering Indians who had run away from Spanish missions. Although the Spanish routinely sent out military expeditions to hunt down and punish these runaways, soldiers were too afraid of the Quechan warriors to dare to venture into the tribe's territory. The Spanish also came to believe that the Quechan and Mojave were involved in a series of local Indian revolts and attacks on Spanish missions and ranches in the region surrounding San Diego

and the Spanish settlement of Los Angeles.

But the only military action the Spanish took against the two tribes was to turn back several small parties of Mojave or Quechan that tried to regain access to the tribes' ancient trade routes to and from the Pacific coast. The Spaniards in Sonora were too occupied battling the Apache and other Indian groups in the colony to pay much attention to the Colorado River tribes.

The authorities of New Spain were also being challenged by their own subjects. After the impoverished *criollos* (people of Spanish descent who had been born in New Spain) staged a series of successful revolts in the early 1800s, Mexico declared its independence from Spanish rule in 1821.

In the mid-1820s, a Mexican military expedition that was traveling westward through Sonora to the Quechan's homeland learned that the tribe wanted to establish relations with the new republic, probably in order to initiate trade. Hoping to take advantage of the Quechan's apparent change of attitude toward non-Indian intruders, the Mexican government sent another, smaller expedition to Yuma Crossing in January 1826. Lieutenant Romualdo Pacheco and his men spent a month in the region building a post that they hoped would help give Mexican travelers free access to the crossing. But the project was abandoned when another wave of Indian unrest swept the areas to the east and west of the Colorado River. The Quechan joined the anti-Mexican forces and shut off all Mexican traffic at the crossing.

The Quechan, however, welcomed American fur traders who arrived in their lands in February 1827. Among them was James Ohio Pattie. He had narrowly escaped death a few months earlier when his trapping party was attacked by Pima and Maricopa warriors along the Gila River. In retaliation, Pattie and other trappers led by George C. Yount destroyed a Maricopa village and slaughtered about 110 of its inhabitants. The trappers had then traveled down the Gila to its confluence with the Colorado, where a large number of Quechan swam across the Colorado to greet them. The Quechan probably considered the trappers to be allies because the Americans had attacked the tribe's traditional Maricopa enemies. The Quechan traded food with the trappers in exchange for red cloth, with which, Pattie wrote, "they were delighted . . . tearing it into ribbands, and tieing it round their arms and legs."

Pattie and Yount each returned separately to Quechan territory later in 1827, and again both were welcomed. The Mojave were not as friendly, however; apparently Yount and his men somehow had angered them and many other tribes in the area that had earlier been hospitable to Americans. The famed mountain man Jedidiah Smith, who had been well received by the Mojave in 1826, found them most unfriendly when he visited after Yount's group had passed through their lands. The Mojave killed 10 of Smith's men and took captive his Indian wife and another woman traveling with the trappers. Trapping parties continued to come to the Colorado River region for several more years, but they could no longer count on a warm reception from the Indians there. By 1834 the price of furs had dropped so low that trapping was no longer profitable and the fur parties disbanded.

Despite the conflicts between Mexicans and Indians in the region, the Quechan occasionally sent trading parties to San Diego. One group of Quechan purchased Mexican wares there with Spanish coins that had probably been among the goods the tribe seized in its attack on the two Spanish missions in 1781. These coins were far more valuable than the purchases the Quechan made with them, so a few non-Indians dashed to the confluence area hoping to find more of these treasures. They soon came back to San Diego empty handed.

During the 1830s the Quechan became relatively prosperous from trade and abundant harvests. Yet many of

A ferry on the Colorado River at Yuma Crossing in the mid-19th century.

their people died during occasional epidemics that swept the area and in frequent battles against their Indian neighbors. The Quechan lost about as many fights as they won against their enemies the Cocopa and the Maricopa. But allied with the Mojave forces they at last devastated the Halchidhoma, the Kahwan, and the Halyikwamai. By about 1839, the remnants of these tribes had taken refuge with the Maricopa along the Gila. Soon afterward some Quechan rancherias moved north into the Halchidhoma's former lands along the Colorado.

Conflicts with Indians in the region took their toll on the Mexican population as well. To escape the warfare, many left San Diego. In 1830 San Diego's population was about 520; by 1840 about 150 Mexicans were left there.

In 1846 Mexico and the United States went to war over the United States' annexation of Texas and other claims it made on what had been Mexican territory, including California territory. During the war, troops from both sides traveled through Yuma Crossing, but they did not stay among the Quechan for long. When the Mexican War ended with the signing of the Treaty of Guadalupe Hidalgo in 1848, Mexico ceded to the U.S. government a vast amount of territory in what is today the southwestern United States, including the homeland of the Quechan. Mexico, however, had never actually controlled this area, and therefore ceded this land without the legal right to do so.

A few days before the treaty was signed, gold was discovered in California and immediately thousands of prospectors hoping to strike it rich rushed to the region. In 1849 from 12,000 to possibly as many as 24,000 Mexicans and Americans poured across Yuma Crossing as they raced westward. Initially the Gold Rush was a great economic boon for the Quechan. For ferrying the prospectors, known as forty-niners, along with their livestock and supplies across the Colorado River, the Quechan charged money and goods, such as horses, red cloth, clothing, and hatchets. The Quechan prized the prospectors' guns but the forty-niners refused to trade them. Despite their business dealings, the forty-niners and the Quechan did not completely trust each other.

The Gold Rush marked the beginning of the end of the Quechan's control of the crossing. The Quechan's ferrying operation was so profitable that American ferry companies decided to go into business along the river. The Quechan did not welcome this competition. But as soon as they drove out one company, another would arrive to take its place. The Quechan also became angry with their own customers because the forty-niners and their livestock plundered the Indians' food supplies, leaving the Quechan with little to eat.

Although there was some intermittent fighting between the Quechan and the Americans, the tribe remained fairly peaceful. Nevertheless, rumors of Quechan violence toward whites were circulated by Americans who were particularly hostile to Indians. One of the most belligerent of these was lawyer and politician John C. Morehead, who in the fall of 1850 raised the California State Militia Volunteers, a renegade outfit comprising about 125 men. The governor of California ordered Morehead to disband his group of vigilantes immediately, but instead Morehead led the militia to Yuma Crossing and destroyed some of the Quechan's crops and ferries. The Quechan retaliated, and the violence escalated into a full-scale battle. The militia soon retreated, taking refuge in a small fort that had been built nearby by some of the American ferry operators. The Indians then also left the battlefield. When Morehead received a second order to disband his force, he and his militia returned to Los Angeles, happy "to get back with a whole scalp to the settlements again," as an American ferry operator recalled.

The incident sparked the United States Army to take military action against the Quechan. Three companies of infantry arrived at Yuma Crossing about three weeks after Morehead's renegades had left. The army commander, Major Samuel P. Heintzelman, proved to be a great enemy of the Quechan. In 1851–52 his troops deliberately did to the tribe what the Spaniards unintentionally had done through arrogance and miscalculation: They destroyed the Quechan's rancherias and crops. Heintzelman's men conducted surprise raids on the Quechan from Fort Yuma, which the American army had built at the crossing atop Indian Hill, where one of the doomed Spanish missions had stood in 1781. The Quechan warriors fought skirmishes with the invaders, but the years of incessant war with their neighbors had so thinned the Quechan's ranks that they lacked the numbers to overwhelm the American soldiers in a mass attack against them.

Even the Colorado River became the Quechan's enemy when in the spring of 1851 it did not flood the Indians' lands. The resulting food shortage was probably more to blame for the Quechan's ultimate defeat in October 1852 than the tribe's lack of fighters; there were still enough Quechan warriors to battle with the Cocopa and the Maricopa for the next five years. It was not until the last large all-Indian battle occurred in the region in September 1857 that the Quechan's military forces were completely annihilated by the Maricopa and their allies.

Major Samuel P. Heintzelman. After his troops defeated the Quechan in 1852, Heintzelman incorrectly predicted that "the vices of contact with the whites will cause [the Quechan] to dwindle rapidly away, and another race will soon occupy their places."

For the 30 years after Major Heintzelman's troops built Fort Yuma, Americans in the region were primarily interested in keeping control of Yuma Crossing, just as the Spaniards had been. Heintzelman proudly described the importance of the location for steamboats traveling up and down the Colorado and as a crossing point for a future coast-to-coast railroad. As long as the Quechan remained peaceful and gave Americans complete access to the crossing, the army was content to leave them alone.

But the U.S. government, again like the Spanish, believed that in order to keep the Quechan at peace it needed to control their leaders. The Americans therefore tried to wield authority over the Quechan by supporting tribal leaders who were sympathetic to their government's aims. In 1852 Heintzelman deposed a kwaxót and a prominent kwanamí as a punishment for launching an attack against U.S. soldiers. Later he appointed a man named Pasqual as the principal tribal chief, to the disappointment of several other Quechan who were clamoring for the position. Dream power, benevolence, bravery, and eloquence remained important leadership qualities to the Quechan, but the government wanted only leaders who would follow its orders.

Chief Pasqual, although placed in power by Heintzelman, was generally respected by his people as well as by the federal government. When the crossing was still under Quechan control, he had been a rancheria leader and an important war leader; he therefore must have had the traditional Quechan requirements for leadership. But Chief Pasqual soon learned to mete out punishment as the Americans did, and he ordered all drunken Quechan to be flogged in public.

In the mid-1850s, a small town was established on the banks of the Colorado River across from Fort Yuma. At first it consisted of only a blacksmith shop, a general store, and a saloon. But by 1858 the town had become a station on the Butterfield stagecoach route into California; by 1873, it was serving as an important stop for steamboats on the Colorado; and by 1875, the town had become the location of a depot on the southern route of the transcontinental railroad. Initially called Colorado City and later Arizona City, the town became known as Yuma in 1877.

Some Quechan began to frequent both the fort and the growing town in the late 19th century. Working in Yuma as woodcutters, janitors, servants, and in other low-paying jobs, these Quechan were exposed to the seamy side

Two Quechan men wearing rabbit-skin cloaks, with an unidentified white visitor in 1862.

A group of Quechan men and women gathered outside a laundry in Yuma in the late 19th century. The men's non-Indian clothing reflects the increasing influence of American settlers on the tribe at this time.

of non-Indian life on the western frontier. Some became involved in drinking, panhandling, and prostitution. Others simply drew their wages and kept to their traditional ways. Most tribespeople, however, avoided the town and continued to farm the river bottomland for their livelihood.

By 1884 the federal government deemed that the Quechan were no longer a threat to U.S. control of Yuma Crossing and instructed the soldiers to leave Fort Yuma. But the relations there between the Indians and the non-Indians were still not entirely harmonious. As had the Spaniards, these

Americans regarded the Quechan as their inferiors. They complained in their newspaper about the drunken behavior of a few of the Quechan who worked in Yuma. Many of the non-Indian settlers who came from further east to live in Quechan territory after the railroad was built across Yuma Crossing had a different concern. They were worried that the Quechan were using too much of the rich river bottomland that they wanted for themselves.

In part to appease the townspeople of Yuma, the Bureau of Indian Affairs (BIA), the U.S. government agency responsible for dealing with Indian pop-

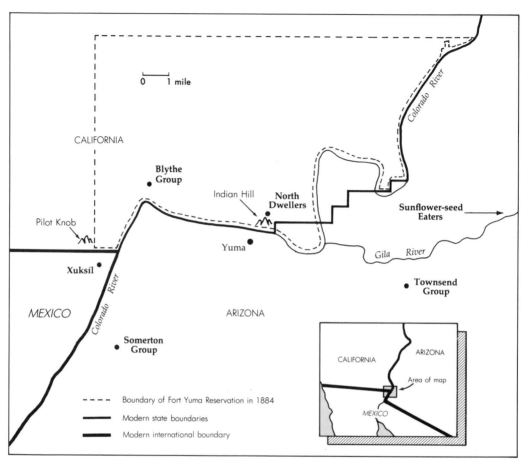

ulations, established the Fort Yuma Reservation as the home of the Quechan in 1884. The reservation consisted of 45,000 acres of land in California on the western side of the Colorado River just across from Yuma. The land closest to the river was fertile, but the soil in the northwest corner of the reservation was alkaline, containing too much salt to be fit for farming. Although the tract reserved for the Quechan was fairly large, it was only a small portion of the territory the tribe had previously controlled.

At this time, there were six Quechan rancherias, each governed by a pa?ipá ta?axán, whom the non-Indians called "captain." Three of the rancherias had been occupied by Quechan for several centuries: The North Dwellers was located near Indian Hill; Xuksíl, near Pilot Knob; and the Sunflowerseed Eaters, about 15 miles northeast of Indian Hill. The other three were formed later: The

Somerton Group was established near the present-day town of Somerton, Arizona; the Townsend Group, about six and a half miles east of Indian Hill; and the Blythe Group, which earlier had lived near the present-day city of Blythe, California, and had recently relocated about three miles northeast of Pilot Knob. In 1884 only the North Dwellers and the Blythe Group were within the boundaries of the reservation, so federal officials soon began to try to persuade the inhabitants of the four outlying rancherias to move to the reservation tract. Many Quechan resisted relocating. Several decades would pass before all of the tribespeople were settled on the Fort Yuma reservation.

The federal government's primary objective in creating the Quechan and other Indian reservations in the late 1800s was to gain control of land and free it for use by white farmers, miners, railroad companies, and land speculators. But the government had another, seemingly more benevolent aim: to help Indians assimilate into the mainstream American culture. Federal policy at the time maintained that it would be to the Indians' advantage to give up their traditional ways and adopt the values and behavior of white society. To help Indians make this transition, the federal government placed Indian peoples on reservations where it could easily take charge of their needs. To protect the Indians, the government would act as their trustee, in the same way that a bank becomes a trustee for a young child who has inherited a fortune. As their trustee the United States would control the tribes' economies, educate their people in the ways of white Americans, and supply them with food and medical attention until it deemed that the Indians were capable of managing their own lives and economic resources. Government officials reasoned that this relationship would not last for long because traditional Indian cultures would soon simply cease to exist: The Indians would learn the new customs and see that they provided a better way to live. But until that happened, the government's plan was to take total control of the Quechan—control of their resources and control of their lives. ▲

Polly-sika, Co-Kiva, and O-pel-u-la, Quechan who served as scouts for the U.S. Army during a campaign against the Apache Indians in 1885–86.

THE FIGHT
FOR
THE RESERVATION

The Bureau of Indian Affairs in Washington, D.C., could hardly oversee the Quechan's day-to-day affairs on the Fort Yuma Reservation nearly 3,000 miles away. The BIA therefore gave the responsibility of managing the reservation to an agent, an official appointed to implement federal government Indian policy on a reservation or in a specific region. The Quechan's reservation was placed under the jurisdiction of the Mission Indian Agency, which was near the present-day town of Colton, California, nearly 200 miles northwest of Yuma. At this distance, the agent there could exert little control over the Quechan. The BIA needed a representative of the federal government on the reservation without having the expense of employing another agent; in 1886 it appointed Mary O'Neil, a Catholic nun, to be the superintendent of the Fort Yuma Boarding School, which had been established in what was once the U.S. Army's fort. Although the Mission Indian Agency was officially in charge of the reservation, O'Neil effectively took over its administration.

O'Neil was faced with the first of many administrative crises a few months after her arrival, when Chief Pasqual died during a measles epidemic that took about 100 Quechan lives. Prior to his death, Pasqual had designated Miguel, a leader of the Xuksíl rancheria, as his successor, even though Miguel may not have had the dream power traditionally required of a kwaxót. O'Neil gave Miguel official government recognition as chief, declaring in a letter to the commissioner of Indian affairs in 1887 that Miguel's appointment "would be no infringement of Indian individual or political rights as they prefer that the government should settle their disputes and appoint their chief." In the tense years to come, Miguel would often angrily disagree with O'Neil about what the Quechan preferred, but for now he accepted the title of chief. In return he agreed to help O'Neil make sure all Quechan children attended her school.

But like Pasqual's appointment by the military in 1853, Miguel's designation as chief was opposed by some Quechan—the "older and less progres-

59

Principal Chief Miguel.

This element is bitterly antagonistic to education and anything else tending towards civilization and progress. They are wedded to the ways of their ancestors, which is tantamount to perpetual poverty, ignorance, starvation, and degradation.

With these feelings, O'Neil could not have created a warm, welcoming atmosphere for her Indian students.

At the school Quechan children were taught by Catholic nuns first to speak English, then to read, write, and do arithmetic. They were also supposed to receive instruction in various vocational skills that would help them get jobs as shoemakers, bakers, farm workers, and in other relatively well-paying positions after they had graduated. Students had little contact with their parents. They ate, slept, studied, and worked at the school and were allowed only infrequent visits home. In 1966, Quechan Marie Johnson still vividly remembered her pangs of homesickness when as a young girl she stared out from the schoolgrounds toward her home north of Indian Hill, hoping to catch a glimpse of her parents as they went about their daily chores.

Quechan parents soon became anxious about what was going on in the school. There were rumors of punishment that was considered harsh by Quechan standards being meted out by the nuns, although such severity was not unusual in public schools for non-Indian children at this time. The nuns

sive element of the tribe," according to O'Neil. This faction was led by José, the leader of the Townsend Group rancheria. His people felt that he would make a better tribal chief than Miguel, and they wanted nothing to do with the new school. O'Neil's description of José's supporters reveals her prejudice against traditional Quechan culture, sentiments that were widespread among other non-Indians at the time:

sometimes whacked young Quechan's hands with rulers; years later, one former student recalled being forced to wear a ball and chain on his legs.

Parents were also angry about the poor vocational training the students were receiving. Instead of being trained for skilled jobs, the children were made to wash dirty dishes, clean and scrub the school, and perform other menial tasks. To the proud Quechan, this was an insult. They took their complaints to Chief Miguel.

A student at Fort Yuma Boarding School in 1890. The teachers at the school required Quechan children to cut their hair and to dress in the clothing of non-Indians of the period.

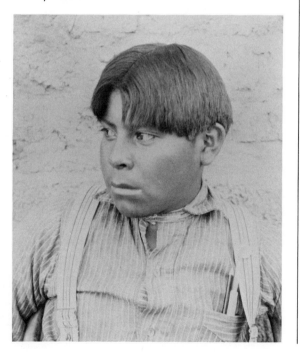

Unlike Pasqual, whom the military usually left alone as long as he kept the peace, Miguel found himself in a difficult situation almost from the day that he was officially appointed chief. José's faction continued to oppose both Miguel and the school. Other Quechan stopped sending their children to the institution. Miguel finally decided to side with his people and refused to help O'Neil round up absentee students.

Meanwhile another issue was beginning to antagonize the Quechan. In 1887 Congress passed the General Allotment Act, also known as the Dawes Act, and the federal government started dividing reservation land throughout the United States into individual plots, one of which was then given to every person in a tribe. The allotment policy was intended to give Indians more incentive to farm their lands, because the government believed that they would work harder on their own plots than they would on tribally owned fields. In addition, allotment opened up more land for non-Indian settlement. After all tribespeople had been assigned a tract, the government usually claimed the right to sell any surplus land on the reservation.

A federal official in California first recommended allotment on the Fort Yuma Reservation in 1890 because, in 1888 and 1889, the Colorado River had not flooded, and the government had to rush $3,000 worth of food supplies to the Quechan to stave off famine. The official argued that if the Quechan were

Quechan schoolgirls, photographed about 1890.

each given a 10-acre plot of reservation land with an adequate supply of irrigation water, the Indians would not be as dependent on the whims of the Colorado or on government aid.

In 1891–92 government land surveyors and engineers arrived on the reservation, and rumors immediately began to spread among the Quechan that their land would soon be allotted. Chief Miguel and one of his most faithful supporters, Walter Scott, lodged a protest against the survey. Miguel and Scott were ignored until they hired white lawyers to prevent the government from surveying their land.

Shortly thereafter, Mary O'Neil and a group of discontented Quechan ousted Miguel from his position, seven years after his appointment. The Mission Indian agent allowed one faction of the Quechan to designate Joe Palma, the son of the late Chief Pasqual, as the new chief. Palma agreed to carry out the government's wishes.

Ex-chief Miguel, as he became known, chose to challenge his dismissal. He traveled around the reservation to build up political support among the Quechan by explaining that as chief he had always acted in the tribe's best interests. On May 12, 1893, he wrote a letter to the commissioner of Indian affairs that implied that Chief Palma was merely a puppet of the government. Miguel also issued a warning:

> Now I speak the truth, if the Yuma tribe want some other chief, I say all right. But I say no one but the Yumas can make a chief of the Yumas. If there is trouble come, I want you to know how it is.

Meanwhile, at O'Neil's urging, the BIA created an armed police force to patrol the reservation, made up of Quechan men who were loyal to the federal government. The BIA established the force to eliminate illegal liquor trade between Quechan and non-Indians, but Mary O'Neil and other federal officials used them to force Quechan children to attend the school against their parents' will.

In late September 1893, the police arrested former chief Miguel, Walter Scott, and six other Quechan men whom O'Neil designated as "troublemakers." Scott and four others were publicly lashed with a whip, and then the eight Quechan were sent to the Los Angeles County Jail. The specific charges and circumstances of the sentencing are unclear, but Miguel and his supporters remained in jail for months.

A few weeks after the men were taken to Los Angeles, the tribe was pre-

Maggie Scott, who, with her husband Walter Scott, was among former chief Miguel's staunch supporters.

sented with the government's plan for allotting the Fort Yuma Reservation. Although the timing could have been a coincidence, it seems likely that the government had arranged for Miguel's arrest in order to keep him away from the reservation while federal officials discussed allotment with the Quechan.

The 1893 plan for allotting the Quechan's land was introduced during a series of meetings between tribe and government representatives. It provided that each Quechan would select a 10-acre allotment of reservation land and receive free irrigation water from a series of canals and ditches to be constructed by the government. It also stated that allotments could not be sold by their Quechan owners for at least 25 years, which would give the Quechan time to learn how to handle their own business affairs. Finally, the plan provided the government with the authority to sell to non-Indians any land left over from the reservation tract after all living Quechan had received their plots. The proceeds from these sales were to finance the development of the Quechan's allotments.

Government officials at the meetings pressured the Quechan to sign an agreement. Some did, but many others did not. The Quechan still insist today that the government agents later forged signatures of fictitious people, so that they could claim that the entire tribe had approved of the plan. This alleged deceit would begin a moral and legal battle between the Quechan people and the United States government that would last for the next eight decades.

Miguel and his supporters returned to the reservation after their release from prison in the spring of 1894. Miguel immediately convened a tribal meeting, during which Chief Joe Palma denounced the 1893 "agreement." O'Neil deposed Palma as chief because

(continued on page 73)

Fort Yuma Reservation, photographed in the late 19th century.

MODERN CRAFTS, ANCIENT FORMS

Most of the Quechan art objects found in museums today were made for sale to non-Indian tourists who visited Fort Yuma. Although they date from the late 19th or early 20th centuries, these works often use materials, techniques, and designs that show strong resemblances to those of objects produced by the ancient Quechan and their Indian neighbors.

Perhaps the most distinctive Quechan crafts are hand-modeled clay dolls, which were also made by the tribe's northern allies, the Mojave. These simple forms are similar to figurines dating from A.D. 1000 that have been excavated from the Hohokam site at Snaketown. Quechan artisans added details and expression to their creations by dressing them using various other materials: horsehair wigs, fabric loincloths and skirts, and glass-bead ornaments. The dolls' bodies are painted with the same pigments and designs that Quechan used to adorn themselves for ceremonial dances.

These linear and geometric patterns are echoed in the designs on the Quechan's 19th-century beadwork collars and pottery, both of which were also produced primarily for the tourist trade. These objects, too, recall earlier traditions: Collars had long been part of Quechan women's ceremonial costumes, and their modern ceramic works were made by much the same method the Quechan's prehistoric ancestors used to create utilitarian pottery.

Quechan male clay doll with red and white body paint, 7 inches high, from 1890. Traditionally, the Quechan's loincloths were made from willow bark rather than the woven cloth worn by this figure.

Mojave figurine of a mother carrying her child, 9 inches high, from 1895.

Quechan infant doll in a cradle and blanket made from willow bark, 9 inches high, from 1922.

A male figurine wearing a cloth loincloth and body paint, 7 inches high, from 1922. The doll's waist-length bead earrings are typical of those worn by Quechan men.

A female doll wearing a willow-bark skirt and wool overskirt, 7 inches high, from 1922. The black paint on the chin of this figure and the one to the left represents tattooing.

After the Quechan and the Mojave obtained glass beads from European and American traders, women from these tribes began to string them on cotton cord to make fringed collars, which they wore over cotton or wool capes. The beading technique is netting, in which rows of beads are interlocked to produce a secure, yet open, fabric that is flexible enough to conform to the shape of the wearer's shoulders. All three collars shown here date from about 1890. (The card in each photograph is marked with the item's museum catalog number.)

A Bowl with triangular handle, 3¼ inches high.

A Three-legged vase, 2½ inches high.

The Quechan made their pottery by first placing a lump of clay on an inverted pot and using a wooden paddle to mold it to conform to the shape of the pot's lower half. They then removed the soft clay from the old pot and coiled rolls of clay around the top of this base to build up the sides of the vessel. The pots were smoothed, dried in the sun, painted, and finally fired in shallow pits lined with hot coals. The vessels shown here were made in about 1900.

Pitcher, 9 inches high.

A clay pipe with a bowl in the shape of a dog's head, 2¾ inches long, from 1890. The Quechan did not use pipes in their rituals; these miniatures were probably made for sale.

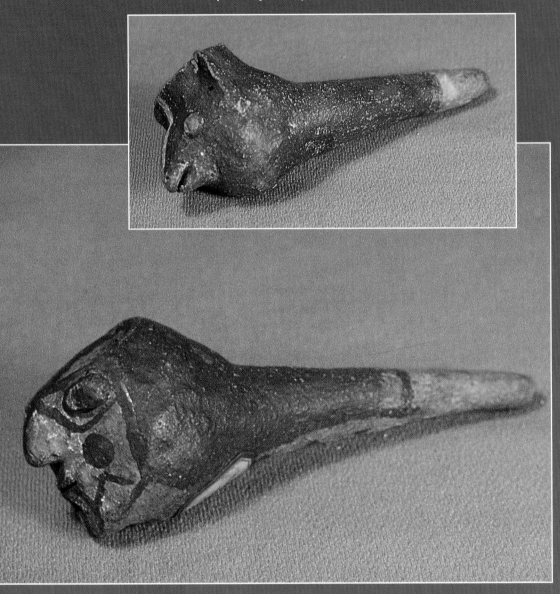

A human-head effigy pipe, molded and painted in the same manner as the Quechan's clay figurines; 3½ inches long, from 1890.

(continued from page 64)

of his statements, and a replacement was not designated for three years. The government now considered tribal chiefs to be relics of the Quechan's past. The government agent, backed by the Quechan police force, in theory held official control over the reservation. Therefore the BIA felt that a chief was not necessary. The Quechan nonetheless demanded official papers certifying one of them as chief of the tribe. Finally in 1897 O'Neil appointed another chief, Pancho LaCherro, from the Townsend Group's rancheria. Not surprisingly, LaCherro was a bitter enemy of Miguel's and a staunch ally of O'Neil's.

Even with LaCherro's support, Mary O'Neil still could not completely control Miguel and his political allies, who had resumed their campaign against the Fort Yuma Boarding School. But now their anger was directed primarily against the overall way in which O'Neil and the government were running the reservation. There were constant confrontations between Miguel's supporters and the police whom O'Neil sent to round up truant students. O'Neil asked federal officials several times to exile Miguel and his "henchmen" (as she called them) from the reservation, but this never happened.

The end of the 19th century was a difficult period for the Quechan. In the past, rancherias had sometimes squabbled with each other, but these disagreements were usually forgotten when the tribe had to band together to battle an enemy tribe. But after the Quechan ceased to fight their Indian neighbors, the people's hostilities began to focus on internal struggles. Political rivals from different rancherias jockeyed for titles and positions that had now become meaningless.

Quechan from the outlying rancherias slowly started to move onto the reservation and settle on land they planned to claim as their allotments. They continued to farm by traditional means, but when the river failed to flood they could no longer stage raids or trade with other tribes to get more food. The Quechan had become dependent on the government for emergency food rations as well as for the selection of their leaders.

Many Quechan were still lured to Yuma despite the government's efforts to keep them on the reservation. Both the Indians and the government became alarmed about the increased amount of drunkenness among adult Quechan. To the Quechan, the wages paid to them by townspeople for unskilled labor also became more important. The Quechan were becoming dependent on the town, just as they had come to rely on the government.

Some non-Indians in Yuma began to take an active interest in reservation events. Both Miguel and his political opponents sought advice and probably letters and petitions from attorneys and other whites sympathetic to their various causes. In this way, non-Indians other than government administrators became involved in reservation politics.

Uniformed ranks of boys marching on the grounds of the Fort Yuma Boarding School. Quechan parents considered the discipline imposed by the school's instructors to be unnecessarily harsh.

One of the most outspoken was J.W. Dorrington, the editor of a Yuma newspaper. He wrote several editorials criticizing Miguel's behavior, the most vicious of which appeared three months after Miguel had lost his chieftaincy and may have contributed to the public support for Miguel's arrest later that year:

> Oh, no Miguel, retire to your lair, repent, reform, and come forth a new Indian, with a new dress, a reconstructed heart, with no brass buttons, but with a cane if you wish, no "G" string or furs, and then we may listen to your tale of woe. It is not quite time for you to assume to run the general government. Just at present Washington is too well posted on your case, to more than courteously listen to what you have to say. Your assault upon the press, because it publishes the facts in your case, and which could have said much more, and truthfully; your attack upon the management of the school, upon the worthy Mother Superior [Mary O'Neil] and her able associates, and your manifestation of a revengeful spirit against others, are entirely uncalled for, and place you in a worse position than you were before. You have picked up this fight, and we throw you down our gauntlet.

The Fort Yuma Boarding School also changed the lives of the Quechan. Family relations became strained because Quechan schoolchildren lived away from home for most of the year. The nuns' efforts to teach young Quechan the ways of white society created even more friction between them and their parents, and the education they received did not prepare them for decent jobs in Yuma. In 1895 even O'Neil admitted in a letter to the commissioner of Indian affairs that the school had failed to assist its students in finding employment:

> I desire to express regret that no encouragement is offered the pupils after graduation. The field of labor here being circumscribed, they of necessity return to the reservation, and retrogression cannot be attributed to a lack of education.

In October 1899 the BIA formally created an agency for the Fort Yuma Reservation. Their services no longer needed, Mary O'Neil and the other nuns left the reservation, and an agent and teachers employed by the government took their place. For the next three decades groups of Quechan would constantly challenge the agency officials' political control of the reservation, just as they had protested the actions of O'Neil.

During this time the Quechan's political factions, each made up of a group of relatives, also continued to battle each other over who should lead the tribe. These groups called public meetings to persuade more Quechan to support them and boycotted the meetings held by opposing factions. They bombarded the agency, the BIA, members of Congress, and occasionally the president with letters and petitions that appealed for the formal designation of a member of their faction as tribal chief. Alliances were often made between some of the factions, but they were always short lived, for alliances changed as the issues changed. All factions felt they were operating for the good of the entire Quechan tribe, but their conflicts were so deep that they could never agree on a single plan to help improve the lives of the Quechan.

Despite the tribe's internal battles for leadership, there was little power to be claimed. The government agent had complete administrative power over the reservation. The Quechan, however, shrewdly came to understand that they could have some influence over agents by complaining to the agents' superiors about their actions. Usually this accomplished nothing in the long run, but the government sometimes would send investigators to the reservation to look into the Indians' complaints, which embarrassed agents who wanted to impress higher officials with their competence. Although this tactic was the only way they managed to wield power, the Quechan behaved as though they had the ultimate authority over their territory. More than 50 years after the Quechan were subdued by Heintzelman's troops, they still refused to act like a conquered people. ▲

A Quechan man plowing the fields on his allotment in 1940.

ALLOTMENT
AND
DISPOSSESSION

Almost two decades after Congress had ratified the 1893 agreement, some Quechan from the outlying rancherias had still not selected their allotments. The government announced that if they did not settle on 10-acre tracts by 1912, it would choose their allotments for them. Many Quechan then set out toward the reservation's eastern boundary in order to claim a tract of the fertile land along the Colorado River. To their surprise and dismay, however, they discovered that non-Indians were already living there.

Without the Quechan's general knowledge, Congress had passed a law in 1904 that declared that all irrigable land on the reservation, except for the approximately 8,000 acres needed for the Indians' allotments, was in the public domain and therefore the property of the government. The 1904 law simply ignored the 1893 agreement, which provided that the Quechan were to choose their allotments before the surplus reservation land could be sold. Federal officials, probably with advice from the

agents at Fort Yuma, put the reservation's richest land up for sale to non-Indians in Yuma without consulting the Quechan. The townspeople eagerly purchased the land directly from the government, without competitive bidding. The price had been set by government appraisal, which did not consider the value the land would have after irrigation. The townspeople knew the government planned to irrigate the land soon, and that they could then sell the property for much more than the price they had paid to buy it from the government.

By 1910 all the best reservation land had been sold, so some Quechan had no choice but to claim allotments on the unfertile semidesert land to the north and west. The Quechan protested the entire procedure when the final assignment of 812 allotments was made in 1912, but there was little they could do. In a 1923 petition to the secretary of the interior, some Quechan recalled how the tracts were formally transferred to their new owners:

In 1912 we were forced to accept allotment though we made our opposition to it. When they would not sign for allotment the Indians had their hands forced down by the Agent to sign or make thumb marks. Nine of our old men who protest[ed] it were handcuffed and the Agent took them to Los Angeles and [had them] thrown into the jail.

By the time the allotment process was completed, the need for irrigation water on the reservation was dire. In 1910 the government had constructed a dam across the Colorado River north of Yuma Crossing. The dam kept the river from flooding the lands on and near the reservation; therefore, none of the soil could be farmed without irrigation. As promised, the government did eventually build irrigation laterals (canals) through both the Quechan's allotments and the reservation land that was sold to non-Indians (known as the Bard District). However, this water was not free to the Quechan, as they had been led to believe during the negotiation of the 1893 agreement. The costs for the lat-

Quechan men rowing across the Colorado River. An irrigation plant is visible in the distance.

erals on both the Indians' and the non-Indians' land were deducted from the Quechan's meager proceeds from the 1910 land sales. Quechan also had to pay for the operation and maintenance of the irrigation system serving their allotments, although these charges were later canceled.

Working poor land, paying expensive water charges, and lacking farm equipment and supplies, a few Quechan nevertheless managed to eke out a living as farmers after the allotment. Most, however, could not. Desperate for cash to buy food for their families, Quechan began to lease their land to non-Indian farmers. But because the federal government was the Quechan's trustee, the allottees could not legally negotiate the leases themselves. Instead the agent set the rent and dictated what the lessee could and could not do with the land. The non-Indians who leased the Quechan's land did not have to pay property taxes or worry about rebuilding the fertility of the soil. Therefore, leasing Quechan allotments was a better deal for these non-Indian farmers than buying land even at extremely low prices.

Unable to farm, most Quechan took menial jobs on the reservation or in Yuma. The reservation school's vocational training still did not prepare young Quechan for well-paying positions in the town or anywhere else. The only income some of the older tribespeople received came from their land leases or from pensions or other forms of government assistance, but this never was much money. After 1912 the Quechan found themselves in the doldrums of poverty. The government's efforts to assimilate the Indians into the American economic mainstream as small-scale farmers had failed, largely owing to the actions of the government itself.

The agents' attempts to force the Quechan to abandon their traditional beliefs and rituals were equally unsuccessful. For example, the agents would not allow Quechan men to enter Yuma unless they had cut their hair short, as white men did. The Quechan were very proud of their long hair. To circumvent the rule, they piled their hair on top of their heads, held it in place by wrapping it with a dark bandanna, and then wore an enormous Mexican sombrero.

The agents forbade the traditional Quechan practice of burning the property of their dead during funerals and mourning services. The Quechan were required to ask the agent's permission to perform ceremonies, and they had to agree not to hold what one agent called "Indian dances, horse races or other harmful features of that character" that were part of their traditional culture. When an agent refused to permit a ritual, however, the Quechan usually held it anyway. In 1922 the Quechan wanted to hold a kar?úk in memory of several Quechan who had fought and died in World War I (1914–18). Agent E. B. Merritt told them that they could have a one-day ceremony, but it would

Quechan Billy Escallante, photographed in the 1890s, wearing his hair in the traditional style. Quechan men were proud of their waist-length rolls of hair and usually refused to cut them despite agents' insistence that they wear their hair short.

have to be performed on Memorial Day, the holiday the federal government had designated for the remembrance of war dead. That year the Quechan publicly staged the first of what would become an annual memorial ceremony patterned after those of non-Indians. They continued to hold kar?úks as well in remote areas of the reservation.

The pressure to assimilate into white culture also restructured the Que-chan household. Households had comprised 10 or more people of all ages who lived together and cooperatively farmed the families' fields, moving seasonally between high ground and river bottomland. After the Quechan had stopped farming, there was no need for a household to contain so many people. Married young adults were no longer needed to work their families' land, so couples who could afford to moved into homes of their own. Children were away at school much of the time, and old people, though still respected, had little to do except mind preschool children and visit friends.

But large households were still economically useful social units. Just as members of a household had pooled their labor, they now pooled their incomes from wages, lease money, and pension payments into a common household treasury. This fund gave the members of the household more buying power than they would have had if each lived on his or her own. But this money was still not enough for them to live decently.

Health problems also took their toll on the Quechan. Although agents tried to keep them from purchasing liquor, alcoholism was common. Tuberculosis, measles, influenza, and diabetes were widespread and often fatal. Until the 1950s, when a small hospital was built on Indian Hill, the nearest hospital that admitted Indian patients for long-term care was 150 miles to the northeast in Phoenix, Arizona. Disease was largely responsible for the diminishing population of the Quechan in the late 19th and early 20th centuries. In 1852 there had been between 2,700 and 2,800 people in the tribe; by 1910 the population had slipped to a low of 834 and did not start to climb again until the 1920s.

Despite their decreasing numbers and extreme poverty in the first decades of the 20th century, the Quechan doggedly clung to the beliefs and values that remained. They had not become economically successful because they could not do so; they had not assimilated culturally because they would not do so.

In this regard the Quechan were not alone. Many other Indian tribes had resisted entering the American cultural mainstream. The federal government, acknowledging its failure to assimilate the Indians, finally reversed its policy in 1934, when Congress passed the Indian Reorganization Act (IRA). This legislation had two important features. First, it ended the allotment of tribally owned land, which had been responsible for much of the Indians' recent dispossession and poverty. Second, it allowed tribes to create their own governments, with constitutions and councils of elected representatives. This new policy suggested that Indian tribes could more easily become part of the mainstream as proud communities rather than as collections of humbled individuals. The government certainly hoped that the Indians' own elected governments could manage reservations more effectively than most agents had done.

The end of the allotment system came too late to benefit the Quechan. They had already lost most of their land. The IRA, however, extended the federal trusteeship over their lands indefinitely, which meant that the Quechan allottees could not sell their tracts. This at least ensured that the Quechan would continue to be the owners of the land that they did hold.

The IRA provided that each tribe would be able to decide for itself whether it wanted to create its own government. Although the Quechan vote was close (129 for, 116 against), in 1936 they agreed to accept a tribal constitution and government by an elected tribal council. Evidently many did not believe that the new tribal government would change their lives for the better. They were probably suspicious of the plan because they had experience with various tribal councils and business committees that agents had set up, all of which had lasted only a short time.

The Quechan constitution provided for a tribal council of seven members, each serving two-year terms. The council would elect the tribal president and vice-president from among its members. Each council member received a very small monthly salary, which ranged between $10 and $20 until the 1960s.

Since the 1880s the Quechan had been battling with the government to gain the power to determine for themselves what should happen in their community. The constitution, which was drafted with the help of BIA officials, could not have entirely pleased the Quechan because most decisions regarding their land and other important issues were still to be made by the secretary of the interior. Nevertheless, the IRA implied that the government had changed its attitude toward Indians. It was now willing to listen to their ideas for improving their own lives.

In 1940 the Quechan tribal council decided to test the government's willingness to listen. It sent a plan through the federal bureaucracy for a cooperative farming venture to improve the reservation's economy. Even after repeated inquiries, however, the council heard nothing from Washington.

The government's failure to respond made it evident to the Quechan that their new government did not have the power to control the tribe's economic life. Soon the people lost all interest in the council. Fewer than half the eligible voters bothered to cast their ballot in the elections. In 1945 a man was elected to the council with just a single vote—presumably his own. At the time some young Quechan adults were probably overseas fighting in World War II, and others had left the reservation to work in defense plants. But even after the war, the Quechan continued to show little excitement over tribal elections or council deliberations.

One important exception occurred in the early 1950s. The federal government had established the Indian Claims Commission in 1946 to rule on claims brought by tribes that sought payment for land and other resources that had been taken from them without just compensation. The Quechan council eagerly filed two claims against the government for the reservation land that had been sold or taken in 1884. After launching the claims process, the council handed over the settlement of the claims to non-Indian lawyers it had hired for a fee of 10 percent of any money awarded to the tribe. For many years, however, the Quechan council and people would receive nothing but occasional reports of the lawyers' slow progress.

Despite the sagging interest in elections and the federal government's continuing domination of reservation affairs, Quechan political factions still had cause to quarrel from time to time. Often the issue was council management of tribal expenses. Although the sums in question were small, conflict over money management was to be expected in a community as poverty-stricken as the Quechan's. Factions not represented on the council tended to mistrust those who were or to chide the council for not fighting hard enough against the government, even when a confrontation would not have accomplished much. This public concern that the tribe was not asserting itself strongly enough in dealing with federal officials showed that the Quechan had still not abandoned their aggressive posture toward non-Quechan authori-

The Yuma Indian Band, which included both Quechan and non-Indian members, in a parade in Yuma, about 1920. In the 1950s, non-Indians were barred from the group, which was later renamed the Quechan Indian Band.

ties. In order to be elected, council members cultivated reputations as fighters who would constantly try to get something for their people, question the authority of the federal government, and watch for any opportunity to seize more power for the tribe.

Throughout the 1930s, 1940s, and 1950s the Quechan continued to be impoverished. By the 1940s small farms throughout the country were no longer economically feasible. They were rapidly being replaced by large, mechanized agricultural operations. The Quechan could not hope to make a living from their individual allotments, while non-Indians who leased a large number of adjoining allotments could do well. The federal government provided no significant aid to the reser-

vation's economic structure during this period. After a brief business boom during World War II, the labor market in Yuma offered few jobs for which Indians were qualified and few that they wished to fill. To make a decent income, Quechan had to move to Los Angeles or another major city, and only those who had the relevant vocational training could hope to find good employment there.

In 1935 the boarding school on Indian Hill was converted to a public day school. Although Quechan parents had been dissatisfied with the school throughout its existence, they were at first opposed to the change. They feared that they could not afford to give their children the same quality of food and other benefits that the boarding

Quechan women selling watermelons they had grown as part of a U.S. Reclamation Service project on the Fort Yuma Reservation in the early 20th century.

school offered. But soon the Quechan parents became active in the public school's management and in school events. For the next 23 years they held most of the elective positions on the local school board. Until 1954 most of the students were Indians. Then the school district was enlarged to include non-Indian children from neighboring areas as well as students from the reservation.

These changes to the school, however, did not improve the preparation young Quechan received before entering the local job market. In fact, stu-

dents were given even less vocational training in the public school than they had received in the boarding school.

The Quechan's poverty continued to grow because of the way allotments were passed on to heirs. When the original allottee died, the tract was divided among the surviving spouse and children. The allottees who had been old when they received their land had long since died. As years passed and their heirs died, the land was subdivided again and again into smaller and smaller portions. Eventually some of the 10-acre allotments were so fractionated that none of the heirs could find lessees for their tiny tracts. Although the federal government encouraged the Quechan to make wills that left the land to a single heir, most did not do so.

In the 1950s the California state government began to exert authority over the reservation. The state administered most of the welfare and other public assistance programs that the Quechan received and was also in charge of the school. In 1953 the state became responsible for law enforcement on the reservation, and the tribe's own small police force and court were disbanded. This was another blow to the tribe's limited authority.

The tribal council was as wary of the state government as it had been of the federal government. The council members were especially upset by California's repeated efforts to tax the personal property of Quechan living on the reservation. According to federal law, the personal property (such as land and homes) of reservation Indians is not taxable. Every time state tax assessors ventured onto the reservation, the tribal council immediately sent irate letters to both state and federal authorities. The assessors were always stopped, but the tribe was irritated that the state continued to completely disregard federal law.

Most frustrating of all to the Quechan was the lack of attention from local, state, and federal authorities to their problems. Their tribal government had supposedly given them a voice, but no one wanted to hear what the Quechan had to say. ▲

Lori Cachora, with the help of the bulldozer behind him, created a barricade in 1974 to protest California state officials' illegal leasing of reservation land to non-Indians.

THE WAR
ON
POVERTY

In 1960, 23 years after it had been created, the Quechan tribal council decided to end its powerlessness once and for all. The council members poised themselves to battle the same issue over which they had fought the U.S. government many times before: control of reservation land. At stake were 4,572 acres of rich river bottomland.

The Quechan's struggle for this tract had begun in June 1920 when the Colorado River flooded so heavily that its waters created a new channel east of the river's old path. Because the executive order that created the Quechan reservation in 1884 defined the reservation's eastern boundary as the Colorado River, the Quechan reasoned that their boundary had moved eastward when the river had changed its course. Therefore, the tribe argued, the 4,572 acres of fertile land that now lay west of the Colorado were properly part of their reservation. The additional land was certainly needed to increase tribal income, so the Quechan soon began to bombard federal authorities with letters

and petitions demanding that they officially hand the tract over to the tribe.

The government said no. The land, it explained, could not be developed or given to the Quechan because it was needed for flood control. But when non-Indian squatters illegally moved into the area and set up small farms, federal officials did nothing to evict them. Every tribal council since 1937 had tried to persuade the government to oust squatters and give the Quechan legal right to the land, but none had succeeded.

The tribal council's furor escalated when the squatters' trucks and cars began to drive through the reservation in order to reach their farms on "the Island," as the exposed tract came to be known. Early in 1960 the council again demanded government action to resolve the land issue. The federal response was noncommittal. Lee Emerson, the council president, finally initiated a public confrontation. He later recalled, "I've seen what unions do, so I suggested, 'Let's do this strike, a good

Quechan deputies guarding the 1960 roadblock.

old American custom.' " Emerson called for the Quechan to blockade all roads on the reservation that led to the Island.

The community was enthusiastic about the plan. The council appointed deputies to set up the roadblocks and wrote to the Yuma newspaper to explain its plan and the reasons for it. Three days later, on April 22, the deputies closed all the roads through the reservation. Many Quechan visited the roadblocks to encourage the deputies and to offer them candy, cigarettes, and food. The blockade continued for four days.

The council's action at last attracted public attention to the question of who

owned the Island. The government offered to return a portion of this area to tribal control. The council refused to accept it, however, declaring that the Quechan had a right to the entire tract. Instead of negotiating further, the government abruptly withdrew its offer. Less than a year after the blockade, it issued long-term leases to the squatters living on the Island. The Quechan had lost again.

Yet the incident showed that decades of poverty and manipulation by outsiders had not destroyed the Quechan's intense desire to control their own community and its resources. Despite the conflict among its political factions, the tribe still had the ability to act as a single unit. The Quechan also discovered a new way of bringing their complaints to the attention of officials in Washington. The government had at least made a small concession to their demands, which it probably would not have done if the Quechan had not staged their protest.

The road blockade was the first in a series of events during the 1960s that would bring sweeping political and economic change to the entire Quechan community. Early in the decade the federal government devised several plans to eliminate poverty throughout the country. Even though these plans were not specifically designed to benefit Indians or to atone for past wrongs the government had committed against various tribes, most reservation Indians were among the poorest Americans, so they would be eligible for government aid. The United States had decided to ease the plight of its poor because the national economy was thriving and the government had money available to spend on social programs. When the national economic picture later turned gloomy, these programs would be cut back or eliminated.

The Quechan welcomed the new federal programs heartily. It looked as though the government was at last going to do something to significantly improve their community. They qualified for programs that were intended to achieve three goals: improve housing and home water supplies, provide bet-

A large billboard along the main road on the reservation in 1966, urging Quechan to participate in programs to improve sanitation.

ter educational and vocational training, and generate jobs for the unemployed. The Quechan would be involved in the planning and operation of all three types of programs. The tribal council therefore would play an active part in producing changes in the community, a position that all Quechan governments had been struggling to achieve since 1884.

The programs were sponsored by various federal agencies, each with slightly different operating procedures and regulations. By working out the details of each program with government officials, the members of the tribal council rapidly learned how various agencies of the government operated and which ones were the best to approach for specific projects. Over time, the council refined its strategy for dealing with federal officials. From the beginning, council members served notice that they were the tribe's official authorities and that they would watch the operation of all programs carefully to ensure that their people were receiving all the benefits the programs promised. The tribal leaders continued to pit their authority against that of outside officials, just as they had ever since the Spanish had tried to secure Yuma Crossing in the 18th century.

Two federal programs called for the eventual construction of 150 new homes on the reservation and a system of water mains and sewers that could bring running water directly into these houses. Until the late 1960s most Quechan homes had no running water.

People drew water from shallow wells in their yards or from irrigation canals. But the irrigation water was so laden with chemicals that it had caused many health problems.

After the government and the tribal council agreed on how the construction programs should be implemented, their operation was to be supervised by a housing authority and a water committee, which included both Quechan and non-Indian members. The two committees were required to submit frequent progress reports to the council.

Construction of the houses and the water system began in 1965. As the programs had been conceived, Quechan volunteers would work on both projects. Although there was a large turnout of volunteers for the first several weeks, soon fewer and fewer Quechan came to participate. The council became frustrated as construction was delayed. Its members, as the community's governing body, sought to take control of the operation of the programs, but the housing and water committees declared that the council had no authority to intervene. The impasse only created further delays in the construction. Eventually the conflict was settled when the federal government abandoned the idea of using volunteers and hired paid construction workers.

The tribal council had fewer problems over the federal programs for education and vocational training. Designated as a sponsoring agency for the Community Action Agency (CAA), the local organization founded by the fed-

Workers on a housing project funded by the federal government in the mid-1960s.

eral Office of Economic Opportunity to supervise most of these programs, the council was directly involved in their operation. The council had the authority to hire and fire the CAA supervisors and workers. Its members also helped work out program plans and objectives.

In 1965 the council hired a talented non-Indian administrator, William Gray, as the director of the CAA. Initially, the CAA focused on what Gray and the council called "soft" programs. These provided information to the Quechan about how they could improve their home conditions and offered classes in basic reading skills. In other CAA programs, Quechan learned the

skills they needed to work as secretaries, carpenters and other construction workers, and teachers. They were taught these skills on the job rather than by attending classes for a long period of time. The CAA also ran a Headstart program that prepared children of preschool age to adjust easily to public school.

The Quechan people were eager to participate in the CAA programs, especially in those that allowed them to receive wages for work as they learned vocational skills. Even though they realized that many of these jobs were temporary, the people welcomed the money. In 1965 the CAA estimated that

170 of the reservation's 180 families had an annual income of less than $4,000. In 1966 the CAA had on its payroll 70 people, most of whom were Quechan. By 1969 the number of CAA employees had increased to 132. The CAA programs were flourishing.

One reason for the CAA's growth was the effective procedure devised by the tribal council and William Gray for dealing with government agencies. In the past the council had communicated with the federal authorities by sending requests and queries by mail through the many levels of Washington bureaucracy. Its members rarely had any face-to-face contact with high officials. Now the CAA had a fund for administrative expenses, which provided travel money for the council members to go to Washington, D.C. They could meet with these officials and present to them in person the council's plans or suggestions for the operation of CAA programs. The council members developed a strategy of explaining what they wanted and how they planned to get it in a clear, businesslike fashion that gained them attention and respect.

Together Gray and the council continued to plan new CAA programs and to apply for money to run them. After about three years they changed their focus to "hard" programs, which involved the construction of buildings and other facilities. These had two important advantages for the Quechan over soft programs: They produced visible evidence that the program money was being used for something practical

The reservation's dancing grounds in 1961.

and they gave the community a chance to begin its own income-generating operations.

One of the CAA's first hard programs trained Quechan as construction workers as they leveled or refurbished all the old buildings on Indian Hill. Through other programs, the Quechan built a shopping plaza, a trailer park, a small youth center, and a large office complex on the reservation. After these facilities were completed, visitors could clearly see that the government's programs had brought about major changes for the Quechan. This type of evidence made it easier for the council to get more funding for new programs.

As government aid to the Quechan increased, so did the council's work load. The tribal council president was particularly burdened. Fortunately the tribe was awarded $520,000 in 1965, when the Indian Claims Commission ruled in its favor on one of the two land claims the Quechan had brought before it. The Quechan eventually received $468,000 after their lawyers deducted their $52,000 fee. The settlement provided enough money to make the office of council president and other tribal jobs full-time, salaried positions.

Three tribal council presidents— Fritz Brown, Henry Montague, and Elmer Savilla—were active in the antipoverty programs of the 1960s and 1970s. During this period, these leaders were political rivals as they vied for the council presidency, which in the 1970s

The dancing grounds in 1974, after a shopping center and trailer park had been built on the site.

became a position elected by the voters at large rather than by the members of the council. Despite very different backgrounds and personalities, Brown, Montague, and Savilla all shared two concerns while in office—keeping the federal programs in operation despite funding cutbacks and maintaining the authority of the tribal government.

In October 1973 President Elmer Savilla made a particularly dramatic display of tribal authority. Without consulting the Quechan council, officials in Imperial County, California, had entered into leasing agreements with non-Indians for a portion of land lying within the 1884 reservation boundaries. To protest these dealings, Savilla and a group of Quechan marched behind a large yellow bulldozer to the area the county had leased (known locally as Sleepy Hollow). They calmly watched as the bulldozer built a low barricade of earth that would keep other vehicles from entering Sleepy Hollow. Savilla's tactic was a replay of Lee Emerson's 1960 road blockade. Like the earlier confrontation, Savilla's plan was to attract the public's attention to the Quechan's land dispute. This time the Quechan succeeded.

Soon after Savilla's march, the government began in earnest to negotiate the return of the 25,000 acres of the original Quechan reservation to the tribe, including part of the Island. Five months later, the government at last agreed with what generations of Quechan leaders had insisted—reservation land had been taken from the tribe illegally. Not until 1983 would the Quechan receive a $15 million claims settlement for land in the Bard District and for the All-American Canal, a large waterway that the government had dug across the reservation in 1938 without the permission of the Quechan. This was the second of the land claims brought by the tribe in the 1950s. Eighty percent of this settlement was distributed to the tribe in per capita (individual) payments of approximately $6,000. The remaining sum was invested, and the resulting interest income was allocated to fund the projects and administration of the tribal government.

Much of the land that was returned to the tribe was rough desert. The Quechan needed irrigation water from the Colorado River in order to make the soil productive. The government, however, refused to discuss the need for irrigation during the negotiations for the return of the land itself. The Quechan were disappointed, but decided to take the land first and to worry about obtaining irrigation water later.

The land negotiations were costly to the Quechan. Members of the council and the tribe's attorney had to make many trips to Washington to hammer out the details of the settlement and to supply information to officials there. The tribal leaders felt the effort and expense were well worth the return of the land. However, they became frustrated and concerned when, after they had at last completed the negotiations, the

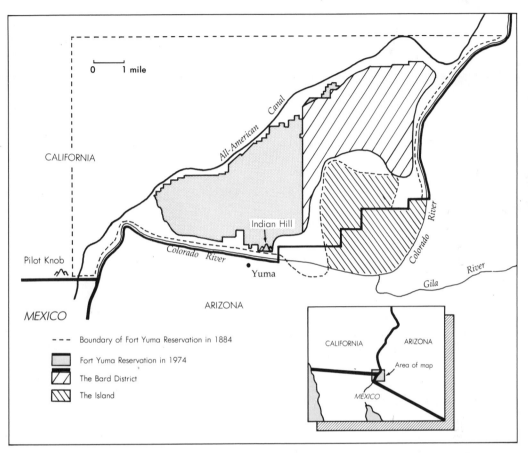

government was slow in granting its official approval of the agreement. Finally in December 1978 the secretary of the interior signed his approval and the disputed land became the property of the Quechan.

While tribal leaders battled the land case in Washington, D.C., in the early 1970s, the council recognized that more changes were needed on the reservation to effectively fight the Quechan's poverty. Although the wages paid through the CAA and other programs temporarily increased the standard of living for many Quechan, the vocational training they provided was not sufficient to guarantee that the CAA workers could find good jobs off the reservation. The government also had begun drastic cutbacks in funding for vocational training, so the Quechan could not depend on funds being available to initiate better programs of this type. Despite the appearance of pros-

The interior of the hydroponic tomato farm.

perity that the new buildings gave the reservation, only the shopping plaza promised long-term employment opportunities for the Quechan, and it provided jobs for only a few people. Yet all the federal programs had so improved their living conditions that the Quechan were hesitant to leave the reservation in search of jobs. The council therefore concluded that it needed to create a source of a large number of good, permanent jobs on the reservation itself.

William Gray and the council decided to turn to the enterprise that had traditionally been the Quechan's economic mainstay—farming. With the

help of Lorraine White, a Quechan who was then the agent at Fort Yuma, and of federal officials they had come to know from their visits to Washington, tribal leaders created two programs that they hoped would make farming on the reservation profitable. They anticipated that when these two projects were in full operation, they could provide jobs for as many as 75 workers.

One project called for the construction of an indoor hydroponic tomato farm. Crops grown hydroponically are rooted in water enriched with chemical nutrients rather than in soil. The Quechan would not need a large amount of land for this type of farming. The council believed that the Quechan could produce two harvests of tomatoes annually in a climate-controlled hydroponic complex.

The other plan was for the development of a large open-air cooperative farm. It would start on a fairly small scale on a 600-acre field that the tribe had leased from the government in the disputed Island area. As the operation grew, it would lease allotment tracts from individual Quechan until all of the reservation's productive land became part of the farm. As a cooperative venture, the outdoor farm would be owned and operated by the tribe as a whole. All Quechan would be able to purchase the food it produced at low prices. The allottees would receive both lease income and a share of the profits from the sale of the crops. Those who worked on the farm would receive wages. By 1975 both the hydroponic and the outdoor farms were in operation.

By the mid-1970s most Quechan were optimistic about the tribe's future. Their various political factions, however, did not agree on what the future should bring their people, so the Quechan's internal conflicts still simmered. But despite their arguments, no one contested that the quality of life on the reservation had improved considerably over the previous 15 years. The federal social programs had given the Quechan higher incomes and better homes, but they had also made the tribe more dependent on the U.S. government and its aid. To continue to prosper, the Quechan recognized that they would have to break free from their economic dependency. ▲

George Yuma, his wife, and their two granddaughters outside their home. Today as in ancient times, the relationship between Quechan grandparents and grandchildren is close.

FORT YUMA TODAY

The future that had seemed so bright to the Quechan in the 1970s came to look much dimmer in the 1980s. Farming, which had served them so well for centuries, had appeared to offer them their best chance at achieving economic independence. But by 1987 both their hydroponic and open-air farm projects had failed.

Several circumstances combined to destroy these enterprises. In 1976 a tomato blight hit the hydroponic farm and ruined the harvest. At about the same time tomatoes and other produce from Mexico became available in local food markets. Because of lower wages and production costs in Mexico, farmers there could grow, pack, ship, and deliver produce to markets in the Yuma area for less than it cost the Quechan merely to grow its tomatoes. The Quechan operation could not afford to price its produce low enough to compete successfully with Mexican farms. The open-air farm primarily suffered from management problems, but it was also

victimized by the environment in 1976, when an entire crop of cotton was destroyed by a hurricane.

Neither operation had a sufficient amount of money to help it survive these crises. Some of the funds the tribe had originally set aside for these programs had been spent on the council's expenses during its land negotiations with the federal government. The crises hit the farms before they had been in operation long enough to generate much additional income.

To keep the farms operating, the tribal council took out loans from the BIA, which they hoped to pay back with the earnings from future harvests. The council members also appointed new administrators and developed different management strategies for the farms. But in the late 1970s the local costs of farming climbed, and the sale of the crops did not bring in enough money to pay back the loans. For several years the tribe continued to borrow more money to save the programs. Finally federal creditors stopped providing loans to the farms, leaving the tribe with large debts.

The council then faced the same dilemma that their ancestors had faced in the early 1900s. They were in possession of valuable farmland but they had no money to develop it themselves. The Quechan arrived at the same solution their ancestors had—leasing their farms to non-Indians. Although leasing provided the Quechan with some immediate income, it was not the most profitable use of their natural resources. The total amount of money made from these leases was small in comparison with the profits the tribe would have made if the open-air farming cooperative had operated as planned. But now non-Indians, not Quechan, would pocket the profits from working the tribespeople's land.

Unfortunately the lessees have had some of the same problems the tribe had in farming the Quechan's fields. Most of them had started their farms with little cash reserve. The rising costs of small-scale farming resulted in profits so low that the Quechan have had difficulty collecting rent from some of the lessees of their property.

Many Quechan families who had leased their allotments to outsiders lost this income completely after the Colorado River flooded in 1983. Despite modern dams and other government strategies for controlling the flooding, the river water overflowed, creating alkaline soil by depositing salt along its

banks and making some land along the Colorado unfit for farming. About a third of the allotments, most of them in the western portion of the reservation, became unusable. By 1987 much of this area was covered with brush.

The failure of the farming operations and the diminishing lease income have been particularly devastating to the Quechan because the government has cut to the bone its funding for anti-poverty programs on the reservation. Quechan work in federal or tribal offices on the reservation or take jobs in Yuma if they can find them. People must still move away from the reservation to find good employment. Tribal officials estimated the unemployment rate on the reservation at 40 percent in 1987. The need for more permanent jobs has yet to be met.

As economic difficulties have returned to the reservation after the relatively good times of the late 1960s, Quechan voters have become increasingly hard to please. Instead of ignoring the council, as the people did during the economic stagnation of the 1940s and 1950s, they now vent their frustration against the tribal government. Petitions demanding the recall of this or that council member are submitted again and again by political rivals who feel that the leaders of their faction could do a better job.

Tribal presidents are now faced with some very difficult decisions. If they decide to initiate radical action to try to improve the Quechan economy, they will be criticized as reckless by their political enemies. If, instead, they play it safe and make few controversial decisions, they will be rebuked for doing nothing to help their people. Either course of action can cost them their presidency.

Perhaps the greatest challenge Quechan leaders must face today is finding new opportunities for economic growth on the reservation. Many Quechan still believe that these opportunities are tied to the land and the Colorado River. The tribe now has land, but it does not yet have irrigation water from the Colorado to make it fertile. The 25,000-acre tract returned to the tribe in 1978 remains almost entirely undeveloped.

The Quechan and other Indian groups along the Colorado are convinced that they have a valid legal claim to more river water than they are now receiving. In 1908 the United States developed the Winters Doctrine, a policy based on a Supreme Court decision allocating shares of water to users in the Southwest. The Winters Doctrine and later court decisions declared that Indian communities, before all others, were entitled to the water they needed for their economic development, not only at that time but also into the future. The returned land is worth little as long as it is not irrigated, and therefore the Quechan feel that their needs and their status as Indians qualify them for more shares of water from the Colorado than they presently have.

But water in the American Southwest has become an increasingly scarce

The oldest building on Indian Hill, after it was refurbished by Quechan vocational trainees as a part of an antipoverty program. The building is now a tribal museum.

Quechan Marie Johnson. The Quechan today struggle to keep their traditions alive by learning them from their elders.

and valuable resource. The Colorado's water is already oversubscribed; if all the users legally entitled to river water were to use their full share, there would be no water left. Obviously none of the other users want to see the Quechan get an increased share. In order to do so, the tribe must wage a legal battle against some extremely powerful utility

companies, such as the Metropolitan Water District of southern California, that supply water to the region's farms and cities.

In 1988 the dispute was still in the courts. The tribe has retained legal counsel, and its total legal fees will be high. Like the money the tribe spent to regain control of the 25,000-acre reservation tract, the sum spent on the water case is a gamble. But it is a gamble the tribe must take if it ever hopes to make its land economically profitable.

As the Quechan have continued the battle to regain their natural resources, the tribe has also still fought to hold onto its traditional culture. To casual observers little appears to be left. The Quechan live in modern houses, similar to those of most other Americans. They wear their hair short and dress as non-Indians do. They drive their cars to Yuma to do their shopping in the supermarkets there. After high school they join the military or leave home to go to vocational school or college. They organize baseball teams and go to church on Sunday. They suffer from health problems and high rates of alcoholism and suicide, just as other impoverished American populations do.

But outsiders who wish to look more closely can see that some of the old ways have survived. The Quechan language is still spoken on the reservation. Elderly tribespeople can detect among themselves some slight dialect differences that mark a speaker as a "southerner," that is, one whose ancestors came from the Xuksíl rancheria. Although Quechan is most often spoken by the old people, some young adults are anxious to keep the language alive. This will not be easy. English has been the primary language of Quechan children for years, and it is the only one they hear in school, on television, on the radio, and in movies.

The Quechan remain deeply affected by death and mourning. They continue to cremate their dead with some of the deceased's belongings, despite the efforts of some agents in the 1920s to suppress both practices. The entire kar?úk mourning ritual is no longer performed, in part because of the time and expense involved and in part because few Quechan alive remember the details of the ceremony and its distinctive songs. But from time to time portions of the ritual are performed at the request of those who have lost a loved one. Memorial Day ceremonies now held on the reservation also include some features of their traditional mourning practices.

Occasionally Quechan gather at the reservation's dancing grounds to listen and dance to traditional songs, such as the *pa?ipá* (people). At these events, in the cool of the evening, ranks of men and women shuffle back and forth in time to the sound of gourd or tin can rattles and the voices of male singers.

Dream power may not have disappeared entirely, although it is passing on with the tribe's elderly. In the 1970s there was still at least one effective curer left on the reservation. More recently, an old Quechan-Mojave man reportedly interrupted his conversation with a community worker to ask her if she would like it to rain. Amused but doubtful, the woman said, "Sure. We need the water." He told her to wait until the following day, that he would use his dream power to bring the rain then. When the next day dawned, the official forecast was for clear skies. But soon a large black cloud-bank gathered and poured rain over the reservation.

And the Quechan attitude survives. The Quechan have been known as fighters for centuries. They have worked hard to keep that reputation. After 400 years of contact with non-Indians, they are still fighting for the same things—control of their land and of the river water needed to make it fertile. In ancient times victory in war brought special power that would keep the tribe strong and thriving. Victory in the modern warfare of courtrooms and bureaucracies could well bring the same kinds of results. ▲

BIBLIOGRAPHY

Bee, Robert L. "Changes in Yuma Social Organization." *Ethnology* 2, no. 2 (1963): 207–27.

———. *Crosscurrents Along the Colorado: The Impact of Government Policy on the Quechan Indians.* Tucson: University of Arizona Press, 1982.

———. "Self-Help at Fort Yuma: A Critique." *Human Organization* 29, no. 3 (1970): 155–61.

———. "Tribal Leadership in the War on Poverty: A Case Study." *Social Science Quarterly* 50, no. 3 (1969): 676–86.

Castetter, Edward F., and Willis H. Bell. *Yuman Indian Agriculture.* Albuquerque: University of New Mexico Press, 1951.

Dowd, D. F. *The Twisted Dream: Capitalist Development in the United States Since 1776.* Cambridge, MA: Prentice-Hall, 1974.

Forbes, Jack D. *Warriors of the Colorado: The Yumas of the Quechan Nation and Their Neighbors.* Norman: University of Oklahoma Press, 1965.

Forde, C. Daryll. "Ethnography of the Yuma Indians." *University of California Publications in American Archaeology and Ethnology* 28, no. 4 (1931): 83–278.

Hakluyt, Richard. *The Principal Navigations, Voyages, Traffiques and Discoveries of the English Nation.* 12 vol. New York: A. M. Kelley, 1973 [originally published in 1589].

Harrington, J. P. "A Yuma Account of Origins." *Journal of American Folklore* 21 (1908): 324–48.

Hicks, Fredric. "The Influence of Agriculture on Aboriginal Socio-Political Organization in the Lower Colorado River Valley." *Journal of California Anthropology* 1, no. 2 (1974): 133–44.

Spier, Leslie. "Cultural Relations of the Gila River and Lower Colorado Tribes." *Yale University Publications in Anthropology* 3 (1936).

Sturtevant, William, and Alfonso Ortiz, eds. *Handbook of North American Indians*. Vol. 10, *Southwest*, pp. 86–98, 99–112. Washington, D.C.: Smithsonian Institute, 1983.

Trippel, Eugene J. "The Yuma Indians." *Overland Monthly Series* 2 (1889) Vol. 13, no. 78: 561–84; Vol. 14, no. 79: 1–11.

White, Chris. "Lower Colorado River Area Aboriginal Warfare and Alliance Dynamics." In *Antap: California Indian Political and Economic Organization,* edited by Lowell J. Bean and T. F. King. Ramona, CA: Ballena Press, 1974.

THE YUMA AT A GLANCE

TRIBE *Yuma (Quechan)*

CULTURE AREA *California*

GEOGRAPHY *desert region of southeastern California and northwestern Arizona*

LINGUISTIC FAMILY *Yuman*

CURRENT POPULATION *approximately 3,000*

FIRST CONTACT *most likely Hernando de Alarcón, Spanish, 1540*

FEDERAL STATUS *recognized, reservation community of more than 33,000 acres in California and Arizona.*

GLOSSARY

agent A person appointed by the Bureau of Indian Affairs to supervise U.S. government programs on a reservation and/or in a specific region; after 1908 the title "superintendent" replaced "agent."

agriculture Intensive cultivation of large tracts of land using draft animals and heavy plowing equipment. Agriculture requires a great deal more effort than horticulture.

alkaline soil Land that has a high salt content making it unsuitable for cultivation.

allotment U.S. policy, first applied in 1887, to break up tribally owned reservations by assigning farms and ranches to individual Indians. Intended as much to discourage traditional communal activities as to encourage private farming and assimilate Indians into mainstream American life.

assimilation The conversion or incorporation of a dominated culture into that of the dominant culture.

Bureau of Indian Affairs (BIA) A U.S. government agency within the Department of the Interior. Originally intended to manage trade and other relations with Indians and especially to supervise tribes on reservations, the BIA is now involved in programs that encourage Indians to manage their own affairs and improve their educational opportunities and general social and economic well-being.

clan A multigenerational group having a shared identity, organization, and property, based on belief in their descent from a common ancestor. Because clan members consider themselves closely related, marriage within a clan is strictly prohibited.

colonialism The control by a powerful government over a dependent government and/or people.

confluence The point at which streams or minor rivers join to form, or flow into, a larger river.

culture The learned behavior of humans; nonbiological, socially taught activities; the way of life of a group of people.

dream power The special abilities received during sleep through visits from the spirit world. Dream power was a requirement for holding an official position in Quechan society.

factionalism The division of one group into smaller groups or parties that are often argumentative and self-seeking.

floodplain Level land that is frequently submerged when rivers flood during the spring thaw. This flooding returns to the soil nutrients that are drained every year by cultivation.

Indian Reorganization Act The 1934 federal law that ended the policy of allotting plots of land to individuals and provided for political and economic development of reservation communities.

irrigation Practice by which water is artificially supplied to cultivated fields, usually by the use of ditches and canals.

Jesuit A member of the Society of Jesus, a Roman Catholic order founded by Saint Ignatius Loyola in 1534. The Jesuits are highly learned and, in the 17th century, were particularly active in spreading Christianity outside Europe.

ka?rúk Quechan funeral ritual that commemorated the death of a brave warrior or exceptional leader. The ritual stressed the roles of death and warfare in Quechan society.

kwanamí Quechan war leader who planned and supervised war parties. The position could be held by any man or woman who exhibited unusual bravery and aggressiveness in combat.

kwaxót Quechan religious leader; the kwaxót presided over rituals and requested the assistance of spirits for tribal guidance.

pa?ipá ta?axán Quechan tribal leader, literally translated as "real man." The position was usually hereditary, but the person had to be invested with "dream power" in order to be qualified.

Quechan The Yuma's name for themselves; derived from *xam kwacan* (literally meaning "another going down"), which was the name of the ancient trail that the Yuma followed to their homeland according to their oral tradition.

rancheria A clustered group of settlements in which the Quechan lived during the fall, winter, and early spring. They came to the rancherias from scattered summer settlements so that supplies could be grouped together and distributed more evenly during the harsher seasons of the year.

reservation, reserve A tract of land set aside by treaty for Indian occupation and use.

squatters People who occupy property without having legal title to it.

totem The emblem or symbol of a clan or family, usually the animal or plant with which the family has a special relationship.

treaty A contract negotiated between representatives of the United States or another national government and one or more Indian tribes. Treaties deal with surrender of political independence, peaceful relations, land sales, boundaries, and related matters.

tribe A society consisting of several or many separate communities united by kinship, common culture, language, and such social units as clans, religious organizations, and economic and political institutions. Tribes are generally characterized by economic and political equality and thus lack social classes and authoritative chiefs.

Xuksíl The largest and most permanent Quechan rancheria, whose name means "sand stone."

Yuma Crossing The area where the Colorado River narrows enough for safe passage, making it important to traders and colonial forces. It became a point of contention between the Quechan (Yuma) and the colonial powers during the 18th and 19th centuries (Spain and the United States, respectively).

ACKNOWLEDGEMENTS

I am grateful to the George C. Barker, Jr., Memorial Fund at UCLA, the National Institute of Mental Health, and the University of Connecticut Research Foundation for providing funding for my research among the Quechans. My greatest debt is to the people of the Quechan Indian Nation, who over the years have welcomed me back, patiently explained and re-explained their ways, and graciously corrected my errors. May they thrive.

Robert L. Bee
Mansfield Center, Connecticut
1988

PICTURE CREDITS

The American Federation of Arts, page 31; American Museum of National History, Department of Library Services, Photo by Charles H. Cole, (Neg. #318320), page 26; Arizona Historical Society, pages 53, 83; Arizona State Museum, University of Arizona, Photos by Helga Teiwes, pages 18, 37, 68–72; Courtesy of Robert L. Bee, pages 14, 25, 28, 45, 89, 91, 92, 93, 96, 98, 101, 102; John Carter Brown Library, Brown University, page 41; California Historical Society, Los Angeles History Center, Photographic Collections, page 24; California Historical Society/Ticor Title Insurance Co., Los Angeles, CA, page 21; Ralph T. Coe, *Lost and Found Traditions: Native American Art 1965–1985*, page 31; Museum of Natural History, Smithsonian Institution, cover, pages 65–67; National Anthropological Archives, Smithsonian Institution, pages 20, 23, 27, 32, 54, 59; National Archives, page 76; New York Public Library, Picture Collection, page 34; The Bradley Smith Collection, Archivo de las Indias, Seville, Spain, page 36; The Southwest Museum, Braun Research Library, Los Angeles, CA, pages 12, 22, 51, 60–64, 74, 78, 80, 84; University of Arizona, Library, Special Collections, page 55; University of Connecticut, Department of Anthropology, pages 86, 88; Western History Collections, University of Oklahoma Library, pages 19, 39; Laurie Platt Winfrey, Inc., page 36.

Maps (pages 2, 46, 56, 94) by Gary Tong.

ROBERT L. BEE is professor of anthropology at the University of Connecticut. He holds an M.A. in anthropology from the University of California at Los Angeles and a B.A. and Ph.D. from the University of Kansas. He has written books on the Quechan, federal Indian policy, and sociocultural change, including *Crosscurrents Along the Colorado: The Impact of Government Policy on the Quechan Indians*. He has also contributed articles to several journals on a variety of Native American groups and issues, including "Tribal Leadership in the War on Poverty: A Case Study" and "Self-help at Fort Yuma: A Critique." He has conducted research with the Prairie Bands of the Potawatomi in Kansas and with the Quechan of California.

FRANK W. PORTER III, general editor of INDIANS OF NORTH AMERICA, is director of the Chelsea House Foundation for American Indian Studies. He holds a B.A., M.A., and Ph.D. from the University of Maryland. He has done extensive research concerning the Indians of Maryland and Delaware and is the author of numerous articles on their history, archaeology, geography, and ethnography. He was formerly director of the Maryland Commission on Indian Affairs and American Indian Research and Resource Institute, Gettysburg, Pennsylvania, and he has received grants from the Delaware Humanities Forum, the Maryland Committee for the Humanities, the Ford Foundation, and the National Endowment for the Humanities, among others. Dr. Porter is the author of *The Bureau of Indian Affairs* in the Chelsea House KNOW YOUR GOVERNMENT series.